In Many Wars, by Many War Correspondents

From Our Own Correspondent

JOHN MAXWELL HAMILTON, Series Editor

Illuminating the development of foreign news gathering at a time when it has never been more important, "From Our Own Correspondent" is a series of books that features forgotten works and unpublished memoirs by pioneering foreign correspondents. Series editor John Maxwell Hamilton, once a foreign correspondent himself, is the founding dean of the Manship School of Mass Communication at Louisiana State University and is the executive vice chancellor and provost of LSU.

PREVIOUS BOOKS IN THE SERIES:

Evelyn Waugh, *Waugh in Abyssinia*

Edward Price Bell, *Journalism of the Highest Realm: The Memoir of
Edward Price Bell, Pioneering Foreign Correspondent for the Chicago* Daily News, edited
by Jaci Cole and John Maxwell Hamilton

William Howard Russell and Others, *The Crimean War: As Seen by
Those Who Reported It,* edited by Angela Michelli Fleming and
John Maxwell Hamilton

Seymour Topping, *On the Front Lines of the Cold War: An American
Correspondent's Journal from the Chinese Civil War to the
Cuban Missile Crisis and Vietnam*

IN MANY WARS,

by

MANY WAR CORRESPONDENTS

Edited by GEORGE LYNCH and FREDERICK PALMER

Updated Edition

With a Foreword by JOHN MAXWELL HAMILTON

LOUISIANA STATE UNIVERSITY PRESS

BATON ROUGE

PUBLISHED WITH THE ASSISTANCE OF
the V. Ray Cardozier Fund
DeeDee and Kevin P. Reilly, Sr.

Published by Louisiana State University Press
Originally published as *In Many Wars, by Many War-Correspondents*, by the
    Tokyo Printing Co., 1904
Appendix 1 and Appendix 2 copyright © 2010 by Louisiana State University Press
Foreword copyright © 2010 by John Maxwell Hamilton
Louisiana Paperback Edition, 2010

Designer: Laura Roubique Gleason
Typeface: Adobe Caslon Pro
Printer and binder: Thomson-Shore, Inc.

LIBRARY OF CONGRESS CATALOGING-IN-PUBLICATION DATA
In many wars, by many war correspondents / edited by George Lynch and Frederick Palmer ;
with a foreword by John Maxwell Hamilton. — Updated ed.
    p. cm. — (From our own correspondent)
  Originally published: Tokyo : Tokyo Printing Co., 1904.
  ISBN 978-0-8071-3709-3
  1. Russo-Japanese War, 1904–1905—Press coverage. 2. Russo-Japanese War, 1904–1905—Jour-
nalists. 3. War correspondents. I. Lynch, George, 1868–1928. II. Palmer, Frederick, 1873–1958.
III. Hamilton, John Maxwell.
  DS517.I55 2011
  355.0209'041—dc22

                                                                    2010020281

CONTENTS

CONTENTS

CONTENTS

Some of the Authors

FOREWORD

"There are few people in the world who have more opportunity for getting close to the hot interesting things of one's time than the special correspondent of a great paper," George Lynch, a veteran British correspondent, wrote in *Impressions of a War Correspondent,* published in 1903.[1]

War reporting. It sounded so romantic. A *laissez-passer* into the front lines of news! And for a time it had been, just as Lynch said. Home from the field of battle, the correspondent was a celebrity, his experiences worth a quick book for the armchair adventurer. But the *London Daily Chronicle*'s special correspondent was to learn the year after his memoir appeared that the war correspondent's life was fast becoming one of hard-to-get press passes and short leashes.

Early in 1904, Lynch and a distinguished throng of foreign correspondents with high hopes of a good story assembled in Tokyo to cover the Russo-Japanese War, only to discover that the authorities were determined not to let them "close to the hot interesting things." Corralled in the Imperial Hotel, the journalists had nothing much to do except tell stories in the bar and scrounge for something to write about. They called themselves "Cherry Blossom Correspondents."[2] In an effort that combined socializing and make-do writing, Lynch and Frederick Palmer of *Collier's* proposed that they and a few of their colleagues join in writing short autobiographic essays about some exciting event in their careers.

The result is this "curiosity of literature," as Palmer called it in a letter to his American publisher.[3] It is not the only instance of correspondents writing reminiscences for a joint volume: others have been assembled. An especially large number were published during World War II. But this one is different because of the circumstances under which it was not only written but also produced. The book was printed in Tokyo in 1904 in a limited number; it was never

The author thanks Lindsay Newport for her research assistance.

published for a mass audience in Britain or the United States, although Palmer hoped it would be. As a result, the book did not find a place on many shelves, which is a pity. It serves up valuable stories not found elsewhere and stands as a signpost on the road to increasingly sophisticated government suppression of information in time of war. Memoirs written after this war would be heavily laced with regrets about what correspondents could not do or see.

●

The Russo-Japanese War had a long fuse. It was lighted by Great Power expansion in the Far East.

For the Japanese, it began when U.S. Commodore Matthew C. Perry forced open their ports in 1854, ending the island nation's isolation. The Japanese were humiliated. The political upheaval that followed brought forth a new generation of Japanese leaders who concluded that they could not recover self-respect by restoring the past. Unable to expel the barbarians, they would emulate them. Japan successfully challenged China's suzerainty over Korea in 1894 and invaded Manchuria. In the resulting Treaty of Shimonoseki, it acquired Taiwan, the Pescadores, and the Kwantung Peninsula in South Manchuria. Although Western powers quickly forced them to relinquish their claims on the peninsula, the Japanese were undeterred. A subsequent commercial treaty gave them the same rights in China as the Western powers enjoyed.

The Russians led the diplomatic effort to force Japan to give up the Kwantung Peninsula. That, however, was not the first sign of the coming clash. In 1860 they created the port city of Vladivostok as a military outpost. Its telling name meant "Rule the East." Russian intentions were also apparent in its railroad building: first the Trans-Siberian Railway, which would make it easier to support their Asian frontier; next the Chinese Eastern Railway, which passed through coveted Manchuria. Three years after forcing Japan to give up Kwantung, the Russians claimed the much-disputed region for themselves and built the South Manchurian Railway, which would connect its rail lines to the Chinese ports of Port Arthur and Dairen.

In response to an Anglo-Japanese Treaty and other diplomatic maneuvering against it, Russia agreed to a phased withdrawal of forces from Manchuria—and then stalled. Adding to Japanese concerns, it sought permission from the Koreans to build a rail line through their country. Recognizing that the Russians were buying time in order to complete all the work on their rail system, the Japanese launched a surprise attack on the Russian Pacific Squadron at Port Arthur on February 8, 1904. The war was on.

Incomplete rail faculties and poor military leadership led to a string of Russian defeats. The Russians lost Port Arthur in January 1905. Japan defeated them in the Battle of Mukden shortly thereafter. In May the Japanese destroyed the Russian Baltic Fleet in a spectacular victory in the Tsushima Straits. The czar, beset by domestic revolutionary threats, sued for peace. The Treaty of Portsmouth gave Japan the Kwantung Peninsula and the South Manchurian Railroad, and recognized its "paramount interest" in Korea. Not long afterward Japan established a protectorate there.

For the first time in modern history, an Asian nation defeated a European one. The Russo-Japanese War brought other firsts that changed the geopolitical equation. As with most wars, there were advances in the art of killing—the first use of machine guns, trench warfare, torpedoes, and cruiser deployment. Also there were firsts in foreign reporting. By some estimates, the Russo-Japanese War was the most expensive to cover up to that time. This was due in part to improved—and costly—communications.[4] But the most notable journalistic landmark of all was not an advance but a retreat. If any conflict marked the end of the Golden Age of war reporting celebrated by George Lynch, this was it.

By most accounts, the dawn of this Golden Age was the Crimean War, fifty years before the Russo-Japanese War. The press in Great Britain and the United States, as well as other countries, was emerging as a powerful political force. More and more commercial enterprises that served readers rather than political parties, newspapers sought to provide reliable news. Reporters became independent observers with large and growing audiences. This shift caught British authorities off guard during the Crimean War. The military didn't quite know what to do with William Howard Russell of the *Times* and his colleagues. While the correspondents suffered discomfort because of a lack of logistical support from the military, they enjoyed a high degree of freedom. Their report-ing, which helped bring down the Aberdeen government, highlighted the Brit-ish command's failures on the field and miserable treatment of its troops.

Over time governments and their militaries determined that they had to discipline the press just as much as they did their soldiers. In an article for *Scribner's*, Thomas Millard, an American midwesterner with a strong aversion to imperialism, criticized British censorship during the Boer War. The enemy that "England wished to keep in ignorance," he said, "was civilization."[5] Lord Kitchener deported Millard. The ability to send news quickly by telegraph—which soon became an imperative in the race to get readers—also became a journalistic weakness because the military often controlled those communica-tions links. Furthermore, many correspondents disliked filing bare-bones tele-graphic reports, which were necessary in order to move news quickly and to hold down transmission costs. No more were correspondents "your coiner of striking phrases," lamented the great British correspondent Archibald Forbes in 1892.[6]

Melton Prior, one of the seasoned war reporters who congregated in Japan, commented in 1897 that correspondents "take no small part in the march of civ-ilization, and it would be a grave pity to my mind, were the events on the bat-tlefield and in the camp left to the General or headquarter staff to send home, as they undoubtedly would be written to suit their own views and wishes or those of the Government." Prior's solution, however, boiled down to the same old problem he sought to avoid. He proposed leaving it up to the commander to inform a correspondent "what he is doing or intends to do, placing him on his honour not to telegraph the information till a certain time, instead of the Cor-respondent having to go about to so-called 'back-doors,' and consequently often obtaining a garbled account and forwarding home false news."[7] There was no bright future in expecting generals to provide correspondents with news about defeats as well as victories.

Devising schemes to control correspondents nevertheless was still a work in progress in 1904. Control was uneven and often as crude as William Tecum-seh Sherman's court-martialing of a reporter who had the temerity to write that the general would have won the Civil War Battle of Vicksburg if he had "acted as earnestly and persistently against the enemy as against the press."[8] The verdict by Sherman's military court was a frank suppression of free speech: the reporter was banished from the "lines of the Army."

In the progression of finding better ways to tame correspondents, the Japanese showed they could defeat not only a European military force but also, with gracious smiles and intransigence, a large force of the West's best war reporters. Wrote Willard Straight, representing Reuter's and the Associated Press:

> The air of the Imperial Hotel was a bright blue from early morn to golden sunset. Famous correspondents, veterans of countless campaigns, were held up, bound hand and foot by the dapper little Orientals. . . . The situation was unique in the annals of journalism. A government holding the rabid pressmen at a distance, censoring their simplest stories, yet patting them on the back, dining them, wining them, giving them picnics and luncheons and theatrical performances and trying in every way not only to soften their bonds and to make their stay a pleasant one, but siren-like to deaden their sense of duty and their desire to get into the field.[9]

Realizing that war was in the offing, many newspapers sent correspondents to Tokyo before the Japanese attack on Port Arthur in February. As a sign of what was to come, it was not one of these journalists who broke the news. The first news came from an Associated Press reporter at Chefoo on the Chinese coast. He based his dispatch on reports from passengers on a steamship that had arrived from the battle scene. The Japanese had turned the Imperial Hotel into a well-provisioned prison.

Over the next weeks more correspondents arrived to take rooms in the "Imperial Tomb," as they called the hotel.[10] Fifty or so bedded down there in early March. Estimates of the total number who covered the war from one vantage point or another range as high as two hundred.[11] Most were British and American, but German, French, and Italian journalists came as well. Although foreign reporting was considered a man's business in those days, at least one woman was among them, Anne Vaughan-Lewes, wife of a British naval officer. She reported on the Japanese side for the *Times* of London.

Among the lodgers at the Imperial Hotel, said Frederick Palmer, were "more famous correspondents than were ever brought together under one roof."[12] Richard Harding Davis, square-jawed, handsome, and resplendent in his custom-made outfits, was the iconic foreign correspondent of his age. Jack London, sent by Hearst, was enjoying accolades for his just-published *Call of the Wild*, destined to become a classic. Others, not so well remembered today, were marquee names at the time or destined to be. Palmer and American-born Percival Phillips with the British *Daily Express* were rising to the top in their profession. Scotsman Bennet Burleigh of the *Daily Telegraph* was already legendary for his audacity and resourcefulness. An American Supreme Court justice who had been involved in Burleigh's imprisonment during the Civil War (Burleigh fought on the Confederate side) professed to be following events in Asia for news of some "wild adventure" from the correspondent.[13] Another bold *Daily Telegraph* correspondent, Ellis Ashmead-Bartlett, had been imprisoned by the Greeks in the Greco-Turkish War of 1897. Luigi Barzini was there for *Corriere della Sera;* Edward F. Knight, who lost his arm covering the Boer War, for the *London Daily Post;* and Thomas Millard, whom Kitchener had expelled and was destined to be one of the more famous China Hands, for the *New York Herald*. Another who would become a fixture in China was W. H. Donald, an Australian reporting for several papers in his country as well as the *China Mail*, where he was an editor. He went on to become an advisor for Sun Yat-sen, whom he helped write the proclamation for a new government in 1911, and other Chinese leaders. A biography of him was titled *Donald of China*.

Davis, Palmer, and many other correspondents wrote nonfiction on the side. Some like Jack London and John Fox specialized in novels. Although Fox's work has not endured, he was successful in his day. One of his more famous novels, *The Trail of the Lonesome Pine*, was adapted for the stage and film. Will Levington Comfort, representing several American papers, also wrote novels and is remembered for his interest in the occult.

Others were known chiefly for their work in visual reporting. Since the Ashanti War in 1873, artist Melton Prior had been covering battles for the *Illustrated London News*. He is memorialized in the crypt of Saint Paul's Cathedral. James H. Hare was the first great daring combat photographer. His maiden overseas assignment was for *Collier's* during the Spanish-American War. Many more wars followed. Richard Harding Davis was to say, "No war is official until covered by Jimmy Hare."[14]

Fewer correspondents were stationed on the Russian side, whose front was much farther from its national capital than the Japanese forces were from theirs. The correspondents in that group included novelist and poet Maurice Baring, who represented the *Morning Post;* Richard Henry Little, who jumped temporarily from the *Chicago Tribune* to the rival *Daily News;* and Francis Mc-Cullagh, who reported for the *New York Herald* and the *Manchester Guardian.* War correspondents representing the Associated Press, as its corporate bulletin noted, included Lord Brooke, "the talented son of the Earl of Warwick, and several well-known Russians. Mr. Kravschenko, the eminent painter and literatteur [*sic*], who served the *Novoe Vremya* during the Boxer troubles in China, was engaged by the General Manager of The Associated Press in St. Petersburg in February and took his departure for the Far East early in March."[15]

The correspondents with the Russian forces had a little something of the old-time freedom with which to operate. "Once a correspondent did obtain permission from the Russians to go to the front," Lord Brooke remarked, "he had practically carte blanche, he could go to the firing line and get himself killed if he chose."[16] AP General Manager Melville Stone, seeking to expand the reach of this service, secured permission from the czar to send news freely from any place in the country, except the front. "They turned over to us in St. Petersburg, daily, without mutilation, the official reports made to the Emperor and to the War Department."[17] Of course correspondents had complaints. Brooke and others were loudly unhappy with censorship in the war zone and weary of being under suspicion. Douglas Story, a Scotsman who represented the *Daily Express,* lamented the rise of censorship in Russia and elsewhere as "a crisis in the affairs of correspondents which must lead to change."[18] But in his memoir, *The Campaign with Kuropatkin,* he had kind words as well as complaints for the Russian censors and remembered one with whom he socialized as "a friend."[19]

The correspondents on the Japan side of the war did store up such fond memories of their press handlers. Burleigh spoke of "the leashed life of a war correspondent with the Japanese,"[20] and so did most everyone else. The Japanese kept them from the front on the pretense of protecting them. The only time the Japanese told the truth, said Richard Harding Davis, was "when they said we would not be allowed to do something we wanted to do."[21] "We are treated like children, nuisances and possible spies," John Fox wrote home in May 1904.[22] Douglas Story, who had been with the Japanese before becoming the first foreign correspondent accredited with the Russian Manchurian Army, said that a "free press was as much a marvel in Japan as a mastodon in Hyde Park."[23]

Melton Prior ranked as the dean of the correspondents by dint of his long career on battlefields. A friend commented that the war "nearly broke his heart."[24] It was to be his last. Prior's communications shortly after arriving in 1904 capture the aggravation:[25]

- FEBRUARY 17. "This is an excellent hotel, with such a nice manager. . . . A meeting has just been held by the correspondents at the request of the Government to settle about our transport in the field."
- FEBRUARY 23. The Japanese "are awfully secretive about everything and frightened to death at our giving away the movements of troops. . . . The Rothschild of Japan, a Mr. Mitsui, head of the house of Mitsui, gave us correspondents a great dinner at the Mitsui Club on Sunday last, the 21st, followed by a magnificent entertainment, with conjuring, dancing (Geisha girls), and a short Japanese play."
- MARCH 15. "There is absolutely no excitement here, and nothing of interest to sketch; it is maddening. . . . You can never get a direct Yes or No out of a Jap; he says it would not be polite, so he equivocates, and humbugs you."
- MARCH 20. "The Emperor opened the Parliament here in person to-day, and we Pressmen were allowed to be present. It had been for some time very doubtful whether we should, but this morning, about two hours before the ceremony, we received our passes. We all had to go in evening dress. . . . Really it is a disgrace the way we are being treated. They will not tell us anything truthfully, but keep on humbugging us."
- APRIL 15. "Most of the people in the hotel have been or are ill. I was well

enough yesterday to go to a reception at the Shiba Palace ordered by the Emperor as a compliment to the correspondents. . . . We had a gorgeous luncheon with every kind of wine, and the royal footmen to serve us. . . . I am afraid the office must be very upset at not receiving sketches, but that cannot be helped, and we are all in the same fix."

• MAY 5. "You must nearly be as sick of seeing, by the above address, that I am still here as I am. Is it not shocking to think that I have been a comparative prisoner in this town for over three months!"

Maybe because the Japanese worried that their restrictions on correspondents were beginning to damage relations with the British and the United States, whose support they wanted, they allowed sixteen correspondents to join Japanese forces in April.[26] Two similarly small groups went later. Seeing any real fighting nevertheless remained a problem. Battles took place on vast Manchurian fields, sometimes obscured by tall millet and kowliang. Worse, the Japanese still weren't interested in coverage. Only after much pleading were correspondents even received at military headquarters. "The Great System," derisively wrote Palmer, who was with the first group, "decided that one correspondent might come from their 'compound' each day and get the news for all. This was like standing outside the inclosure and having a man on the fence tell you who has the ball on whose fifteen-yard line."[27] "Your prophecy concerning the dearth of telegraphic news has been verified beyond your fondest hopes," Willard Straight wrote to his AP boss, Martin Egan, "—there has been nothing worth a message."[28]

Not until the end of July was Prior "off to the front" with the second group. "It is true we are at the front, with the enemy within four miles of us," he wrote at the end of August, "but—and this is a very big 'but'!—we are simply prisoners within these city walls, and if we very particularly wish to go outside we have to make special application, and an officer is sent to accompany us; but of course we are not allowed to go near the troops or outposts, or see anything to write about or sketch."[29] Four correspondents in the second group—Richard Harding Davis, John Fox, George Lynch, and Prior—missed a major battle because their Japanese liaison officer told them it would not take place. From time to time Censor T. Okada came to inform correspondents, "All is going according to plan." "Don't forget to tell us if it's not," said Jack London.[30]

Reports from the field went though maddening censorship, not once but multiple times. Telegrams were censored at the headquarters and then at other stations. Prior complained that six officers had an opportunity to make deletions before dispatches arrived at Nagasaki or Tokyo. By the time the stories reached England, he lamented, "they were quite unreadable."[31] Besides this, the Japanese were not dependable about promptly sending reports onward. Some stories took five or six weeks to reach home. Some never made it at all.

The Japanese were far from contrite. When he was still in waiting around in Tokyo, Prior spoke to General Fukushima, "our only mouthpiece with the Government." The general said that the first group of correspondents "had given so much trouble and had complained so much that he did not know what to do."[32]

Many who rendezvoused at the Imperial Hotel had known each other for decades. "I have not come across Burleigh yet as he is at Nagasaki, but shall do so, I hope, very soon," wrote his old campaign partner Melton Prior shortly after settling in.[33] Many remained thick with each other out of affection and for practical reasons of mutual aid once they were in the field. But as time wore on, clouds swept over the festive mood of reunion. After the war, W. H. Donald liked to tell a story about two drunk correspondents who decided to duel each other, an idea that was prevented by a timely earthquake that gave them time to sober up.[34] One reason to hang around with other correspondents, Frederick Villiers of the *London Graphic* noted, was "to keep watch upon one another."[35] None wanted a rival to get an advantage.

One of these prisoners of war most prone to escape was Jack London. Palmer considered him "the most inherently individualistic and un-Socialist of all Socialists I have ever met and really, I thought, a philosophical anarchist."[36] He "preferred to walk alone in aristocratic aloofness, and always in the direction he chose no matter where anybody else was going." Just four days after arriving in Japan, London broke out of the Imperial Hotel, taking the train to Moji, where Japanese police arrested him for taking pictures in an unauthorized place. After the American ambassador intervened, London hired a junk that took him to Korea. With another renegade correspondent, Robert Dunn, who was reporting for the *New York Sun*, he managed for several weeks to get color stories of life in the field, although nothing close-up of the fighting. In early March 1904 the Japanese put him in a military prison and subsequently attached him to a group of correspondents in Seoul. His final run-in with authorities occurred when he punched a Japanese groom whom he suspected of stealing fodder for his horse. He was arrested awaiting courts-martial. Honoring the code that correspondents help each other, even if the reporter in need is not all that comradely, Richard Harding Davis contacted President Roosevelt, who arranged to have London freed upon the condition that he go home. London was happy to give up writing about "the woes of correspondents, swimming pools and peaceful temple scenes."[37]

If London's freelancing irritated them, correspondents did what they could to escape, too. Jimmy Hare slipped away to get stunning pictures of the Battle of Yalu in May. Palmer was on his own for a couple of days when his conducting officer did not meet him as planned during the Battle of Liaoyang. The Italian reporter Luigi Barzini managed to get a good look at the Battle of Mukden at the end of the war.

There was freelancing at sea as well. Before the war started, the *Times* of London made arrangements to deploy a new technology to get a jump on news.[38] Lionel James hired a streamer, the *Haimun*, equipping it with a wireless transmitter, and erected a 180-foot-high mast on the China coast to receive its messages. The *New York Times* shared in the cost and benefited from resulting stories. News he sent of the Japanese blockade of Port Arthur and their landing at Darien was significant. So was a story that the competitive James euchred from a London *Daily Mail* correspondent. The correspondent had been eyewitness to a battle scene on the Manchuria-Korean border that the Japanese would not let him report. James took him aboard the *Haimun* and offered to help him find a cable station, then transmitted the stories himself by wireless. To ensure the *Daily Mail* correspondent was fully out of action, James liquored him up and locked him in his cabin.

Correspondents in Tokyo were miffed that James enjoyed a competitive advantage and sought to level the playing field by urging Western officials to lodge protests to the Japanese. Although James did not admit it for some years, he had made a deal with the Japanese to place a putative interpreter on the *Haimun* whose real job was to act as a censor and a spy for the navy. But even that arrangement was not enough. Eventually the ever-wary Japanese scuttled James's scheme, and he was back on land trying to cover the war. Disgusted with censorship restrictions, he eventually went home.[39]

Boats without wireless capability plied the water, too. The *Fawan*, chartered by the *Chicago Daily News*, remained afloat longer than the *Haimun*, but not without tribulations.[40] John Bass, the *Daily News* chief correspondent, took the boat to the mouth of the Yalu River and transferred to a Chinese junk that was to transport him upriver to the Japanese forces. The Chinese skipper, thinking he would get a reward for turning Bass over to the Russians instead, headed in another direction. Once he figured this out, Bass mutinied, steering home with one hand and holding his revolver in the other. At one point the vessel took fire from the Russians. On two other occasions Russians seized the *Fawan*, once arresting correspondent Stanley Washburn. Finally, the Japanese purchased the boat from its owner in order to end its activities.

Correspondents were not far removed from the Spanish-American War, where sensational reporting led to outright fabrication. And as happened in that earlier conflict, competitors liked to unmask colleagues who concocted news. Noted the English-language *Japan Daily Mail* in Yokohama: "It appears, therefore, that the British *Daily Telegraph* employs as special correspondents spooks or spirits, omnipresent, since they can be simultaneously writing messages from Moji in Japan and taking observations on the coast of Korea, and omniscient since they can witness imaginary battles from a distance of over 100 miles. Stranger still is it to find that this wonderful correspondent saw a battle fundamentally different from that which really took place."[41]

The very best long-distance job of faking news may have been a story concocted in Baltimore. News of the last great engagement of the war, the Battle of Tsushima in May 1905, trickled to American papers, and much of the information that did arrive fell into the category of rumor. After several days of this, H. L. Mencken, managing editor of the *Evening Herald,* made up an account rich in detail. The story in the paper's Tuesday edition, May 30, began, "From Chinese boatmen landing upon the Korean coast comes the first connected story of the great naval battle in the straits of Korea on Saturday and Sunday." Mencken considered the story his "masterpiece of all time, with the sole exception of my bogus history of the bathtub."[42] (Mencken's subsequent account of his escapade is wrong in several respects. The dateline of the story was Shanghai, not Seoul, as he said. Furthermore, contrary to another one of his assertions, it was known by the time he wrote his story in the *Herald* that the Japanese definitely had won. But why would one expect any more fidelity to truth in Mencken's latter account than in the first?)

By the end of 1904, the number of correspondents covering the war had dwindled. Palmer, who went home for a while, came back the next year to see the final Battle of Mukden. Of course he could not take in much. While waiting around for something to happen, he and Robert Collins, an AP man, asked each other from time to time, "Have I ever told you" some personal story or another? The response, said Palmer, was "'Yes, you have, you babbling fountain of prolix repetition,' or something like that."[43] Tale spinning, like the reporting, wore thin.

●

In Many Wars, by Many War Correspondents was born in the Imperial Hotel at a time when the correspondents were, if stymied, still hopeful. It is full of the sorts of stories that correspondents were regaling each other with in the hotel bar.

Details about the book are as hazy as the morning-after memories of a boozy night.[44] In his memoir, Melton Prior spoke of plans to have a local Japanese printer produce an *edition de luxe* to sell for a guinea (twenty-one schillings) and an ordinary one costing five schillings. There seems to have been discussion of the one version appearing in both English and Japanese. Also

Palmer wrote his publisher, Scribner's, proposing that it bring out the book in the United States, but it apparently was not interested. A copy of the English-language version printed in Japan is near impossible to find today. The one that forms the basis for this book was purchased from a London book seller and may be the more elegant edition, if indeed two versions were printed. The book has a cover of very fine cloth. The gilt title on the cover seems to be hand painted. A silk cord binds the book. I have left the text untouched, including the typos. The reader will note authors' signatures at the end of some of the stories. The correspondents signed small slips of paper that were pasted into each book.

The correspondents hoped the book would make money, but not for them. "It is said we ought to clear at least £2,000," Prior speculated in early March, "but I believe we shall make much more."[45] The banking firm that had put on a party for the correspondents, Mitsui & Co., acted as treasurer and took up subscriptions. The proceeds were to go to a relief organization, the "Teikoku Gunjin Yengokwai," for the benefit of those who were orphaned and widowed by the war. While the humanitarian gesture had a nice ring to it, one expects it was cynical. It could not hurt to curry favor with the authorities.

The correspondents' personalities and humor come through in these pages. They tell their stories in different ways—prose, poems, pictures, and even a short play. "How shall I ever write it?" asks artist Grant Wallace's war correspondent, facing a blank page headed "My Most Interesting Experience." An Italian correspondent writes a dreamy romantic story in his native language. A Frenchman, in a similarly flowery account in his tongue, tells of his hopes of reaching Korea, where the action was. Translations of both are found in appendices.

Despite the title, not all of its stories are about wars or even journalism. Martin Egan tells a boyhood tale about a narrow escape from a rattlesnake bite. One of the authors, Sir Bryan Leighton, may not have been a journalist at all.[46] "He is an interesting man," the wife of the Belgian ambassador wrote in her diary in March 1904, "fond of adventure, and I fancy has come out here as an amateur war-correspondent."[47] Sir Bryan is the lone author not to have a news organization attached to his name in the table of contents. Yet most of the book is devoted to correspondents' routines, failures, and triumphs. AP correspondent Sam B. Trissel describes his kit: "I find I have procured everything except a pianola, alarm clock, ice-cream freezer, lace curtains for the tent, chestnut roaster, easy chair, umbrella, and a safe deposit vault for the dog." Franklin Clarkin of the *New York Evening Post* captures the roiling emotions of reaching "the little corrugated zinc cable-house solitary on a knoll[,]" where he and his colleagues could file their stories, only to be let down when they were informed that the way station in Halifax could not handle them. The biggest triumph for a war correspondent, of course, is to stay in the saddle and alive, a point made more than once. "I had lost my spurs," writes Will Levington Comfort, "and it is a harsh thing to think now, but I kept the pony on his feet by stabbing his flanks with a leadpencil [*sic*]." In response to the request by Lynch and Palmer to "Give us your most exciting war experience," George H. Kingswell of the *London Daily Express* begins, "Here's mine, I nearly died with the Irish Brigade in Natal."

And, yes, there are stories about what Percival Phillips calls the "Campaign of the Imperial Hotel." London recounts his first arrest in Japan. In the chapter written as a play, which takes place on the "Veranda of the Imperial Hotel, Tokyo," bewhiskered correspondents learn that the war "ended thirty-nine years ago! And the War Office never told us!"

⬤

One reason for Japan's victory was, as Thomas Millard reported, "a carefully matured plan, carried out thoroughly and with remarkable attention to details."[48] As effective as Japan was at planning and executing the war, there wasn't any evidence that restrictions on the press made any great difference in the outcome. Correspondents were adamant that they would never report information that would give away vital information to the enemy of the forces they were with. In his memoir about the war, even the "wild" Bennet Burleigh insisted, "What a creature that correspondent would be who would betray the host with whom he remained as an honoured guest!"[49] Yet nothing was lost as a result of constraining correspondents either. Russian General Alexi Kuropatkin, looking for scapegoats, pointed to the press in his memoir. "Many of the correspondents at the front, ill-informed as to our own operations, and worse informed as to the enemy's, did not scruple to dispatch reports founded on entirely unreliable information, and so, by exaggerating the importance of every reverse, shook public confidence still more."[50]

Another lesson of the war lay in Japan's public relations activities. Well before the conflict, the Japanese realized that to be a member of the Great Powers they had to convince the world they were a civilized nation. Management of international opinion also was central to allaying concern about a "Yellow Peril" and staving off efforts to take away Japan's spoils afterward. The Foreign Ministry carried out a study of Western public opinion in the foreign press in 1898. Two years later Japan took more direct steps not only to monitor news coverage in Europe and the United States but also to promote Japanese views. Among other things, they distributed releases to news bureaus under false names. When war loomed, they sent two special envoys abroad, one to Europe and one to the United States, to coordinate what today would be called public diplomacy. "By manipulating the British press," instructed Japanese Foreign Minister Komura Jutarô in February 1904, "we must persuasively explain the righteousness of our cause and help to defend our interests by showing that the Japanese government was obliged to take up arms in self-defense and that Yellow Peril principles are unreasonable, etc."[51] The Japanese took other measures to affirm their modernity. The Japanese Red Cross had the largest membership in the world. It impressed foreigners who had the opportunity to observe the care given to wounded Russians during the war. Ashmead-Bartlett made note of the "desire on the part of the Japanese Headquarters Staff to avoid anything in the nature of an appearance of triumph over the fallen foe."[52]

This worked. Jack London left with ill will toward his hosts, whom he considered "childish" and "savages."[53] John Fox, who carried away "in heart and mind the nameless charm of the land and of the people," hated their "polite duplicity."[54] But sentiment in the United States and Great Britain ran heavily in favor of the island nation. "The opinion prevails here that Japanese diplomacy is comparatively open and trustworthy—more 'Christian' than Christian Russia's," editorialized *Century* magazine.[55] Rev. J. H. De Forrest was well aware of the plight of the correspondents "cooped up in the Imperial Hotel."[56] But that did not overshadow his good feelings about Japanese intentions. "There were no drunken feasts, no geisha girls, no gambling, no demoralizing loafing after the victories, but ceaseless preparation for the next battle," De Forrest wrote in the *The Missionary Review of the World*. "The Japanese are a wonderfully open-minded people, seeking for truth and light in all the world."[57]

These lessons were not lost on political and military leaders in World War I. This was the first total war. Entire societies were mobilized into enormous war machines. This machinery included gears and levers to control what people knew and what they thought, an effort that naturally involved correspondents. Governments organized them, censored them, and fed them information on an unprecedented scale. "Propaganda dates back 2,400 years, to Sun-tzu's *The Art of War*, but the First World War saw its first use in an organized, scientific manner," writes Phillip Knightley in his history of war reporting. "War correspondents were among its first victims."[58]

Many of the authors in this book were part of that conflict. John Bass, Jimmy Hare, and Richard Harding Davis covered the war, the latter, just fifty-one years old, dying in 1916 of a heart attack. Percival Phillips, who acquired British citizenship, was one of the first five correspondents accredited to the British Army on the Western Front. After the war he was knighted, as Knightley snidely puts it, "for his services to his country, if not to journalism."[59] Ellis Ashmead-Bartlett brought forth a story worthy of William Howard Russell, telling of an eyewitness account of the botched British landing at Gallipoli. Commanding General Ian Hamilton, who said the reporter "could not be trusted," lifted his credentials, but it was the general's career that came to an end when an inquiry into the campaign was completed.[60] After the war, Ashmead-Bartlett was elected to Parliament. Robert MacHugh, an Irishman who represented the *London Daily Telegraph*, commanded an artillery brigade in World War I and later worked as a spy, entering Germany dressed as a Spaniard. William Maxwell, knighted in 1919, became head of a section of the British Secret Service. Martin Egan left journalism before the war to do promotion work for J. P. Morgan & Co. During the war he served as an aide to General John Pershing, who commanded the American Expeditionary Force (AEF) in France. (He was a military observer during the Russo-Japanese War.) Egan also kept up his old friendships from the war. Egan had a telephone conversation with Richard Harding Davis minutes before his old comrade died.

What of the editors of this book? George Lynch started out covering the war for the *Westminster Gazette*. Before it was over he founded the Barbed Wire Traverser Company Ltd. His inventions for overcoming barbed wire included special gloves and a quilt that could be used to bridge the sharp obstruction. Frederick Palmer spent a number of frustrating months trying to go into the field with British forces during the war. When the United States entered the fray, patriotism led him to turn his press pass in for an AEF uniform. His job was to manage the press for Pershing, with whom he had struck up a friendship during the Russo-Japanese War. This was not a happy experience, what with correspondents' complaints about not being able to see the first American troops go into the trenches or the first of them buried. United Press correspondent Lowell Mellett said that Palmer, the "censor-in-chief," was "the saddest Major in the U.S. Army."[61]

"I used to have some friends in the army and among newspaper men," Palmer said, "Now I'm suspect to both sides. The army suspects me because I try to convince them there is a lot of stuff that really ought to be printed; the newspapermen because there is a lot of stuff that really ought not."[62]

John Maxwell Hamilton
March 2010

NOTES

1. George Lynch, *Impressions of a War Correspondent,* reprinted ed. (London: George Newnes, 1903; repr., Gloucestershire, UK: Dodo Press, no date), xi.

2. Earle Albert Selle, *Donald of China* (New York: Harper, 1948), 22.

3. Frederick Palmer to Arthur Scribner, March 25, 1904, Archives of Charles Scribner's Sons, Special Collections, Princeton University Library.

4. Robert W. Desmond, *The Information Process: World News Reporting to the Twentieth Century* (Iowa City: University of Iowa Press, 1978), 417–29, identifies many of the correspondents sent to cover the war.

FOREWORD

5. Thomas F. Millard, "The War Correspondent and His Future," *Scribner's*, February 1905, 243.

6. Archibald Forbes, "War Correspondence as a Fine Art," *Century*, December 1892, 294.

7. Melton Prior, "Is the War Correspondent a Necessity of Civilization?" *The Idler*, September 1897, 284.

8. James M. Perry, *A Bohemian Brigade: The Civil War Correspondents* (New York: John Wiley & Sons, 2000), 144.

9. Herbert Croly, *Willard Straight* (New York: Macmillan, 1925), 125–26.

10. Nathan A. Haverstock, *Fifty Years at the Front: The Life of War Correspondent Frederick Palmer* (Washington, D.C.: Brassey's, 1996), 121.

11. Desmond, *The Information Process*, 419.

12. Haverstock, *Fifty Years at the Front*, 122.

13. F. Lauriston Bullard, *Famous War Correspondents* (Boston: Little, Brown, 1914), 194.

14. Cecil Carnes, *Jimmy Hare: News Photographer* (New York: Macmillan, 1940), 131.

15. "The War Staff," *Service Bulletin of the Associated Press*, October 15, 1904, 7.

16. Philip Towle, "British War Correspondents and the War," in *Rethinking the Russo-Japanese War, 1904–1905*, ed. Rotem Kowner (Folkestone, Kent, CT: Global Oriental, 2007), 321.

17. Melville E. Stone, *Fifty Years a Journalist* (Garden City, NY: Doubleday, Page, 1921), 277–78.

18. Douglas Story, *The Campaign with Kuropatkin* (London: T. Werner Laurie, 1904), 64.

19. Ibid., 106

20. Bullard, *Famous War Correspondents*, 228.

21. Richard Harding Davis, *Notes of a War Correspondent* (New York: Scribner's, 1914), 220.

22. John Fox, Jr., *Personal and Family Letters and Papers*, comp. Elizabeth Fox Moore (Lexington: University of Kentucky Library Associates, 1955), 60.

23. Story, *The Campaign with Kuropatkin*, 43.

24. S. L. Bensusan, preface to, *Campaigns of a War Correspondent* by Melton Prior (London: Edward Arnold, 1912), v.

25. Prior, *Campaigns of a War Correspondent*, 320–35.

26. Frederick Palmer, *With My Own Eyes: A Personal Story of Battle Years* (Indianapolis: Bobbs Merrill, 1932), 237. Foreign Ministry officials responsible for following public opinion in Europe and the United States urged a relaxation of press restitutions, which they viewed as counterproductive. See Robert G. Valliant, "The Selling of Japan: Japanese Manipulation of Western Opinion, 1900–1905," *Monumenta Nipponica* 29 (Winter 1974), 431–32.

27. Frederick Palmer, *With Kuroki in Manchuria* (New York: Scribner's, 1904), 223.

28. Willard Straight to Martin Egan, July 14, 1905, Willard Dickerman Straight Papers, Cornel University Library.

29. Prior, *Campaigns of a War Correspondent*, 332, 335.

30. Palmer, *With My Own Eyes*, 239.

31. Prior, *Campaigns of a War Correspondent*, 329–30. Also see Michael S. Sweeny, "'Delays and Vexation': Jack London and the Russo-Japanese War," *Journalism & Mass Communication Quarterly* 75 (Autumn 1998), 554.

32. Prior, *Campaigns of a War Correspondent*, 329.

33. Prior, *Campaigns of a War Correspondent*, 323.

34. Selle, *Donald of China*, 22–23.

35. Desmond, *The Information Process*, 420.

36. Palmer, *With My Own Eyes*, 242. Details of London's wartime experience are found in Alex Kershaw, *Jack London: A Life* (New York: St. Martin's Press, 1997), chapter 9, and Sweeny, "'Delays and Vexation'" 548–59.

37. Sweeny, "'Delays and Vexation,'" 555. See also Robert Dunn, *World Alive: A Personal Story* (New York: Crown, 1956), chapter 8.

38. Peter Slattery, *Reporting the Russo-Japanese War, 1904–5* (Folkestone, Kent, CT: Global Oriental, 2004), 37–38, and passim; Gavin Weightman, *Signor Marconi's Magic Box* (Cambridge, MA: DaCapo, 2003), chapter 24; Desmond, *The Information Process*, 421–24. A first person account is David Fraser, *A Modern Campaign: Or War and Wireless Telegraphy in the Far East* (London: Methuen, 1905).

39. Valliant, "The Selling of Japan," 437.

40. The *Fawan*'s adventures are described in Charles H. Dennis, *Victor Lawson: His Time and His World* (Chicago: University of Chicago Press, 1935), 268–71.

41. "Feats of Reporting," *Service Bulletin of the Associated Press*, September 1, 1905, 4.

42. Baltimore *Evening Herald*, May 29, 1905; H. L. Mencken, *Newspaper Days: 1899–1906* (New York: Alfred A. Knopf, 1941), 272.

43. Palmer, *With My Own Eyes*, 259.

44. Prior, *Campaigns of a War Correspondent*, 324; Haverstock, *Fifty Years at the Front*, 122.

45. Prior, *Campaigns of a War Correspondent*, 324.

46. Sir Bryan, ninth baronet, was a military man with a passion for horses and wars. On his own initiative, he went to Cuba in hopes of joining the American forces in the Spanish-American War. He did not find a place in the military, but rode around a good bit, thanks to the foresight of having brought his own horse. He was in the company of correspondents

from time to time, and one history mentions in passing that he wrote for the *New York Journal*. He later was on hand for the Boer War and, after the Russo-Japanese War, with the Turks in the Balkan War. He commanded a regiment during World War I and was an early proponent of military aviation. Although his journalism status is in doubt, his poem ("Waiting and loafing and drinking and smoking/Honestly (?) earning our pay!") is very much in the sprit of bona fide correspondents in Tokyo. Sir Bryan's Cuba adventure is described in E. Ransom, "Baronet on the Battlefield: Sir Bryan Leighton in Cuba," *Journal of American Studies* 9 (April 1975), 13–20. The passing reference to him as a correspondent is in Charles H. Brown, *The Correspondents' War: Journalists in the Spanish-American War* (New York: Scribner's, 1967), 361.

47. Baroness Albert d'Anethan, *Fourteen Years of Diplomatic Life in Japan* (London: Stanley Paul, 1912), 366.

48. Thomas F. Millard, "The Fighting in Manchuria," *Scribner's,* October 1904, 412.

49. Bennet Burleigh, *Empire of the East: Or Japan and Russia at War, 1904–5* (London: Chapman & Hall, 1905), 446.

50. Alexi Kuropatkin, *The Russian Army and the Japanese War* (New York: E. P. Dutton, 1909), xviii. The Japanese were just as hard on foreign military observers. As Palmer notes, "The tactics of the World War were predicated in the Russo-Japanese War. The attachés wanted to see the operations of the infantry from the contact to the taking of a position in order to know the effect of quick-firing, long-range weapons. This the Japanese would not permit. Their public reason was that foreigners might be mistaken for Russians by Japanese soldiers in the heart of combat. But [Major-General] Fujii gave me the basic reason when he said: 'We are paying for this information with our blood.'" Palmer, *With My Own Eyes,* 248. The restrictions on foreign military observers are discussed in J. N. Westwood, *Russia Against Japan, 1904–05: A New Look at the Russo-Japanese War* (Albany: State University of New York Press, 1986).

51. Valliant, "The Selling of Japan," 423.

52. Rotem Kowner, "Becoming an Honorary Civilized Nation: Remaking Japan's Military Image during the Russo-Japanese War, 1904–1905," *The Historian* 64 (Fall 2001), 30.

53. Sweeny, "'Delays and Vexation,'" 554.

54. John Fox, Jr., *Following the Sun-Flag: A Vain Pursuit through Manchuria* (New York: Scribner's, 1905), 187, 189.

55. "American Sentiment Concerning Russia and Japan," *The Century,* September 1904, 816.

56. J. H. DeForest, "War News from Japan," *Independent,* April 7, 1904.

57. J. H. De Forest, "What I Found in Manchuria," *The Missionary Review of the World,*

November 1905, 849–50. The spelling of the author's name varies in the two publications.

58. Phillip Knightley, *The First Casualty*, rev. ed. (Baltimore, Johns Hopkins University Press: 200), 85.

59. Knightley, *The First Casualty*, 190.

60. The comment on Ellis Ashmead-Bartlett is from a report in the files of the American Expeditionary Force, Field Censor to Chief, C.2.D, March 2, 1919, Record Group 120, Entry 228, Box 6132, National Archives.

61. Mellett's quote is from a story that he wrote about the problems of censorship, which was recorded in an AEF memorandum, D.C.C. (for Mr. Hurley), December 15, 1917, Record Group 120, Entry 239, Box 6211, National Archives. Palmer liked Mellett, whom he often visited in Washington after the war "just because he makes me feel better." Palmer, *With My Own Eyes*, 374.

62. AEF memorandum, D.C.C. (for Mr. Hurley), December 15, 1917.

PREFACE

WHILE many war correspondents were waiting in Tokio to go to the front with the Japanese army, the idea was suggested and readily taken up, that each should write a short story of one of his most interesting experiences. The entire proceeds of the sale, the authors decided, should be devoted to the "Teikoku Gunjin Yengokwai," association for the relief of those serving in the Army and Navy. The objects of this society are:

To give assistance to those who come under the following classification, always however, with due consideration for the relief given by other similar public and private institutions.

Distressed families of men serving in the Army and Navy who are killed or die while on service.

Men serving in the Army and Navy who become cripples while on service, as well as the families of such men, in case of distress.

Distressed families of men serving in the Army and Navy whether at the seat of war, or in fortresses, garrisons, etc. at home.

The authors appeal to, and rely on, the charity and good feeling of publishers not to publish any copy of this edition which the editors have not the opportunity of copyrighting in English-speaking countries.

GEORGE LYNCH.

FREDERICK PALMER.

EDITORS.

Imperial Hotel.
Tokio, May 8th, 1904.

In Many Wars, by Many War Correspondents

A Naval Engagement.

In former days one of the most fascinating features of, and also one of the greatest incentives to warfare, was the prospect of loot it held out to the contending armies. Now all that is changed ; the soldier, his officer, and his general are paid an equivalent in money, for what a grateful government considers he would formerly have made by looting from the enemy.

This system is worked out on a calculation—at least it was after the South African War—that the looting capacity of a field marshal was formerly four hundred times as great as that of a private soldier. How far this was true it is impossible to say ; one thing is quite certain, no field marshal has ever refused his share of battu money on the ground that its proportions constituted a libel on his predecessors in that office.

When the Turkish army takes the field, it is a noticeable fact, that the moral tone of everyone connected with it is considerably lowered. An idea seems to be prevalent that you might just as well take anything that comes your way, for the simple reason that if you do not, the next person who comes along will.

Thus I have seen the most respectable members of society and others busily engaged in stripping the interior of a Greek Church, in order to save the Icons from sacrilege at the hands of the infidel.

The Turkish soldier in reality cares little for looting; there are few things he covets, these he takes, all else he passes by. Not so the irregulars who accompany him on his campaigns. The Albanian is a born plunderer, it is his vacation during peace and war. Both the Turks and the Albanians are perfectly justified in their behaviour.

Even if the prospect of battu money were held out to them, the chances of getting it would be so small, that each man might well feel incumbent on him to hold a few articles as security, until his government settled his claim. Also, whether the Turk looted or not, he would always be accused of it by the rest of Europe. The old belief that a Christian, however bad, must of necessity be better than a good Turk, dies hard.

After the capture of the Maluna Pass by the Turkish army under Edhem Pasha, the Greeks took up a position in the plain of Thessaly, some 18 miles from Larissa. The morning fixed for the assault, while the troops were taking up their allotted positions, it was suddenly discovered that no enemy existed to attack. The evening before some irregular cavalry attached to the Turkish army had wandered close to the Greek lines. Their appearance had caused a panic; the whole army fled precipitately in the direction of Larissa, the rear protected by some war correspondents, who could not realise the necessity for such a sudden departure. The panic did not stop at Larissa; the mob of soldiers, camp followers, spectators, war correspondents, and inhabitants of Larissa itself, passed right through the town and finally came to a halt at Valestinos and Volo.

When the Turks entered the town Larissa was practically deserted, except for the scum of the gaols, who had been released and were engaged in looting the houses, the credit for this achievement being subsequently bestowed on the Turks.

The Europeans attached to the army were allotted empty houses by the Provost Marshal. The occupants of the house in which I had quarters had evidently left in a hurry. The floor and bed were strewn with articles of clothing, scent bottles, hair pins and handkerchiefs. On the following day I found out that this house had been the residence of the Crown Prince and Crown Princess of Greece. Prince Constantine at that time commanded the army; the panic had overtaken the Prince and Princess so suddenly that they were only just able to get away in time, leaving half their baggage behind.

Under these circumstances I thought it would be justifiable to carry away a few articles as souvenirs and made a selection, which included among other things a dress. These I annexed, that I believe is the polite word used in war for what constitutes robbery in times of peace.

Some months later, the writer, in company with the late Sir E. Ashmead Bartlett, M. P., returned from the front. The bridges over the River Peneaus having been destroyed, it was necessary to skirt along the coast in a small sailing ship, laden with corn, and manned by Greeks. We rather suspected the sailors of treachery so kept a careful watch on them during the night to see that they sailed in the right direction. One morning, when six miles from our destination Platamona, we found ourselves becalmed. Three little clouds of smoke right down in the horizon marked the track of some steamer. This seemed greatly to interest our crew. They talked among themselves ; we asked what it all meant. " Nothing. Italian men of war," was the answer given us. Warships they certainly were, and coming up fast. We urged the sailors to get out the sweeps and row us ashore ; this they refused to do. A closer acquaintance showed the strange vessels to consist of a gunboat and two torpedo boats, but of what nationality it was impossible to say. No flag was displayed. They circled round our devoted little craft training their guns on her. The gunboat ran up the Greek flag and an officer in excellent English invited us to surrender as prisoners of war, without further resistance, as the consequences would only be disastrous. This latter remark seemed to me a quite unnecessary sarcasism.

We politely but firmly declined to surrender and go on board the gun-boat. This upset all their calculations; they had not reckoned on a refusal. The senior officers held a conference ; this lasted some time but no decision was reached ; finally a book of rules was produced, in it a passage was found evidently meeting the requirements of the situation.

The gunboat supported by the torpedo boats, moved towards our little ship ; for a moment I thought it was her intention to ram us, so close did she come. But no ; they preferred to take us by boarding. Twenty-five sailors, armed with rifles and fixed bayonets, and led by an officer, dashed upon the deck cheering loudly. They seized our baggage and commenced to search the vessel, proding the corn with their bayonets, under this all my loot was concealed. Rifles, swords, helmets, pictures and ornaments were all brought to light and handed up into the gunboat, finally the precious parcel, containing the property of the Crown Prince and Princess was produced. A Greek sailor untied it, glanced at the contents, then flung it down on the deck with a gesture of contempt, at the same time making some remark which caused his comrades to laugh.

I suppose it was " Chercher la temme " or its equivalent. " Ah, you villain," I thought, " if you only leave that parcel and dress alone you may have everything else with pleasure." Leave it he did and I seized the first opportunity to conceal it.

They next tried to induce us to follow our baggage on to the gunboat. We refused absolutely to leave the sailing ship. The Captain begged us to yield to the inevitable as he had no desire to use force, he pleaded in vain; and in despair returned to his own ship. What was the poor man to do ? His first act was to summon the senior officers of the torpedo boats to another conference. At length a decision was reached. A rope was fastened to the mast of our vessel, a sailor placed over it as sentry, steam was got up, the torpedo boats took up a strategical position on either flank, the whole flotilla steering for Volo. The sea had meanwhile risen, what force could not accomplish the motion of the boat could. I felt my resolution gradually deserting me, the big, comfortable gunboat looked so very tempting from our small boat catching the full benefit of the wave thrown up by her screw. Knowing that my father would never give way, I thought it best to surrender unconditionally without consulting him, so waved a white handkerchief. This signal was understood ; the screw stopped, willing hands hoisted us on board, our captivity had commenced.

President McKinley's Assassination.

During the afternoon of September 8, 1091 I stood, with five fellow reporters, on a raised platform under a stained glass window in the Temple of Music at the Pan-American exposition in Buffalo, New York. In front of us the chairs had been angled to form an aisle from one door to the other and at the apex of the aisle stood William McKinley, receiving.

The light was subdued and from the pipe organ welled the solemn music of Bach. Much as lumbermen propel logs with cant hooks at a spring drive, the soldiers of the marine guard were pushing the people of the streets up the aisle to the apex and out through the opposite door. It was a solvent setting for the climax of a tragedy. There was the chief of a great nation, a glorious architecture, a sublime religious anthem ; against this came a rabble representing the human undergrowth of millions.

The crowd—sweaty, coarse, dull—had been filing through in fitful sluggishness for less than an hour when I heard two shots, one like the hit, the other like the miss of a cap pistol. Before me the floor became suddenly chaotic. The deed was as a flash of forked lightning in summer, when one moment all is serene and beautiful, the next a giant oak, shattered and ugly, proclaims a ghastly end. President McKinley lay in the arms of the Exposition's president, moaning, fumbling red-dabbled fingers across his bared bosom. He had been shot in the chest and stomach. On the floor in front of him sprawled a bloody fanatic, with eyes glaring in tigerish satisfaction, shrieking a defiant laugh, and a bold curse : " I have done my duty." In a frenzy of remorse and rage, the detective who had let him pass was trying to kick off the assassin's head. With bayonets on their muskets, obscenely swearing, the marines were pricking some of the people in driving them from the temple.

Not this, but later, when I realized what it meant, was the most dramatic moment I have lived, for I saw the assassination of a President of the United States.

Through the following two weeks of gloom, a gloom that lay over the civilized world like a pall, I followed the body of the murdered man. There were eight days of weary waiting, in alternate hope and despair, for the end. When the wan pulse had ceased, Theodore Roosevelt, the President-to-be, made his fervid, startling declaration to stand by the policies of the martyred statesman. Then the world stood still while a nation buried its dead.

What a burial it was ! As we passed on the funeral train from Buffalo to Washington, from Washington to Canton, the States stood by as silent sisters draped in black to honor him whose memory alone could be honored. At the White House, the admirals and generals of the United States accompanied the casket to the East room, where the body lay in state.

Pennsylvania Avenue was in a drizzling rain. The skies seemed weeping. I rode in a carriage with General Otis. From the windows people could be seen lining the broad way, canopied by umbrellas. A dog yelped. A man jerked off his coat, threw it over the dog, seized the hairy, discordant throat in a grip as of steel fangs and choked out a mongrel life. Then, with hat off, his eyes filmy, the rain bathing him mistily as in tears, the man watched the procession, the dog dead at his feet. So, six weeks later, in an electric chair, the assassin was hustled from existence.

The pace of that return of death to the home of triumph was slow, the silence more intense than absence of sound ; it was the dirge prayer of millions, unvoiced. From ahead came the muffled beat of drums, indistinct through the rain, like a dream. This sublimation of a national sorrow, pervasive as death, eternal as mystery, melancholy as the minor chord of music underlying the joy of all peoples, can never be forgotten. It was a moment in which, looking back, a man finds that his soul leaped forth to the unknown.

Nor can be forgotten the entry to Canton, when behind the casket marched the President, the leading senators and foreign ministers, and, in full uniform, their breasts glittering with decorations, the generals headed by Miles and the admirals by Dewey. In front came the veterans of the

23d Ohio, Civil War heroes of whom William McKinley had been one. The crowd was packed on each side of the street until from a height it seemed a carpet woven of humanity. The town's population had been three times doubled. Again the pace was slow, the silence absolute. The sun shone mellow, the air was cynically clear and cool. The stillness was pierced by one note only—the mournful plaint of a flute as it caroled, " Flee As a Bird."

The next day, under the upshoot of a shaft of granite where it assembled the mist of a sullen afternoon, I saw the body laid away forever, while a new President stood near, with that prescient die across his past and in his face the rapture of a high resolve.

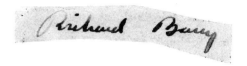

From Our Special at the Front.

Roving knights of the pencil,
    Jolly smooth blades are we,
In ruck and luck of camp and march,
    On intravenal sea.

Ping of wire in our rifles,
    Boom of mail from our mounts,
We fire at sight, and sight to fire
    World echoes from our ' founts.'

Old World's a monstrous gossip,
    A babbling dame o' the town;
" O say ! " " D'ye hear ? " " What's that ? " It's from
    Our labial godown.

Blest and curst of the nations,
    Strife sentineis are we,
Of royal tilts as Moltke bred
    To slink of Soudanee.

At the far-flung drama's crux,
    We hardily hold stalls,
Critical. erudite, eager,
    As a nation rises or falls.

Grim in the clash of epochs,
    We mask all cringe at fight;
Nor check nor laud ; tell and let tell
    Of Nihon and Muscovite.

Wait in capital eddy
 The stride of epaulette ;
O, rasp and gash, ye censor blade ;
 Earn the silence ye get !

Up, away in the morning ;
 Pick of peoples at eve ;
Under the stars, with salt of blood,
 We sniff the grub they leave.

What grub for hollow hillsides,
 Ghastly, common and sore :
What purge of the rank earth's sourness
 In sacramental gore !

Soldierly dash and danger,
 None of a soldier's pay :
We dare and risk, we flare and flout,
 All we can do is—say !

Under the Fire of an International Fleet.

Fifty men of war, the watch dogs of the European Powers, dragged at their chains with the ebb and flow of the tide in Suda Bay. In full view, less than three miles distant, the Turkish block-house Malaxa stood on the edge of an arid plateau, outlined against the sheer, dazzling walls of the White Mountains of Crete. On three sides of the block-house the Cretan insurgents lay, rifle pressed against jowl. These black-bearded men in voluminous trousers were gathered in groups wherever a depression, ridge, or bolder, offered cover. In the centre of each band was planted its standard. They were mountaineers, the descendents of men who, during three centuries, had fought for independence, and they in turn had bound about their heads the black handkerchiefs of rebellion; rebellion against the injustice of Turkish rule.

Rifles cracked from the loopholes of Malaxa and bursts of smoke ran the length of the wall, but in vain; for the eight centimeter guns of the insurgents were out of rifle range. These guns were hidden from the sight of the foreigners in Suda Bay by a high mound. Jumping back and toppling drunkenly on one wheel, they battered away at the thin back wall of the block-house. The foreign monsters lounging on the smooth bed of Suda, seeing only the front of Fort Malaxa, were blind, and in those days that preceded the Greco-Turkish war no one paid any attention to a fusillade in the hills. Only the Cretan insurgents and the besieged garrison knew how serious the fight was.

On the day before the admirals had sent a message to the Cretan chiefs saying that the Great Powers, since they had not allowed the Turks to send reinforcements to Crete, would not permit the insurgents to occupy the Turkish block-houses in the circle of hills. The answer had been this unseen attack on Malaxa.

The plan was made on the night before at a barbecue given to the Cretan chiefs by Constantine Mano, the leader of the Sacred Legion. Mano was an Athenian, a graduate of Oxford, reader to the Empress of Austria, a dilletante in literature and a dabbler in sports. He had come to Crete to join in the insurrection against the hated Turks, just as his father had done before him and as many young Greek bloods used to do. Mano had gathered about him the best fighting men of the mountains. They were tall men, straight of limb and lithe of body. They went over the hills with the ease of mountain goats. My nationality brought me the place of scribe to the band. Oh, the freedom of life of the Sacred Legion, fighting in the early morning, feasting at night, plunging in the cold mountain streams, sleeping under the stars on the moon-flooded hills!

At the feast a council of war was held. The question was settled in short order. The admirals were usurping power. The Christian nations of the earth would not prevent the Cretan Christians from driving the heathen Turk into the sea. Malaxa should be attacked on the following morning. Then, under the flare of the torches they placed a sheep roasted whole on the table. In red wine we toasted the Great Republic and the little island; liberty, equality, fraternity or death. We left the board to take our positions for the fight on the morrow.

For hours the spasmodic fusillade from the fort was answered by the regular discharge of the mountain guns, which at last bored through the wall of the block-house. Shells could be seen bursting on the inside. The insurgents, the Sacred Legion always in the front, drew closer and closer their half circle. On one side, where the hill pitched sharply down towards Suda Bay, the fort had been left uninvested by the insurgents who wished to keep out of sight of the foreign fleet. Suddenly the fire from the loopholes redoubled. The door of the fort swung open. A great shout went up from all the Cretans. Out of the opening a dozen soldiers in blue uniforms and red fezes plunged forward. Bent double they ran for the edge of the hill only fifty feet away. Would they reach it? The Cretan rifles popped like corn over a hot fire. The Turks fell, one after another, until only three remained to throw themselves over the brink and find safety in the valley below.

Two hours passed. I looked from the mound where I sat, down on the valley with its cool verdure of olive and orange trees, over the smooth quiet of Suda Bay and out to the ocean blue that faded into the golden mist of the Ægean. Here was a picture of undisturbed peace. No red line of Turkish fezes came winding among the olive groves, no unusual movement was perceptible aboard the men of war. With shells bursting within and ammunition dwindling the block-house was fast becoming untenable. In vain the bugler of the garrison trumpeted for help. Quarter was never asked or given between Christian and Moslem in Crete. Was the garrison to fall victim to Turkish sloth and European indifference?

A second shout from the Cretans drew my attention to the block-house. There floating beside the Turkish flag I saw a white cloth. Malaxa had surrendered! In an instant every Cretan was on his feet and running towards the block-house. My "striker," or rather man at arms, dropped my belongings and disappeared. I picked up my overcoat, cameras, field glasses, water bottle and sabertash, and hanging them about me, like presents on a Christmas tree, followed.

The crowd packed about the fort were now visible from Suda. On this howling mass the three Turkish gunboats in the bay opened fire; but, owing to their fear of hitting the block-house, they shot high. Already some of the insurgents had climbed the walls of the fort and were thrusting their rifles through the loop-holes. It seems that when the Turkish major saw the excited insurgents coming he made up his mind to keep them out. On their side, the Cretans, maddened at the refusal to admit them after the white flag had been raised, wanted to break in the door. Mano, with the Sacred Legion, wishing to save the lives of the garrison, stood at the still closed door between the Cretans and the panic-stricken Turkish commander, trying to argue with both. The shells from the Turkish gunboats came about two to the minute; and as they passed with the whirring sound of a great saw cutting the length of a log, the shouting mob were dumb and bowed in low silence. Forthwith they rose again, shouting, jostling, trying to drive Mano from the door.

The situation was desperate. Each moment the insurgents, became more unmanageable. Mano's eye, in search of some expedient, wandered over the turbulent horde and by chance fell on me standing apart. He beckoned. It looked like an impossible road to travel, but as if by common consent strong arms shoved me along. Before I knew it I was standing by Mano's side. . The hubbub was so great that although Mano shouted I could not make out what he said. Then one of those silence-bringing shells passed over us. In the lull he said:

"We shall all get killed if this keeps up. See what you can do with that old fossil inside."

The pinched, white face of the Turkish major was pressed against the bars of the wicket in the door. I got as close to the opening as I could and waited for a lull. It was unpleasant speaking with those shells buzzing over head. The major seemed to find confidence in the presence of a foreigner.

"Why don't you open the door?" I shouted. "If you hesitate any longer they will shoot you through the loopholes."

"Won't we be killed any way?" he asked.

"This man and his followers," pointing to Mano, "will do what they can to save you."

"Shall I open the door?"

"Yes."

"I'll let you two in."

The bolts were drawn and the door opened just wide enough to admit us both. Mano disarmed the Turks, stacked their rifles near the door and placed the prisoners at the further end of the enclosure.

"You stand in front of them with your revolver," he said.

Then he opened the door and called in about twenty of the Cretan chiefs. There was some wrangling about precedent, but, on the whole, matters went smoothly enough. The chiefs divided the rifles and handed them out to their followers. I looked about me. There were a number of Turkish dead laid out along one of the walls. About half of the garrison of two hundred men were wounded. A captain with a bandage over one eye rolled a cigarette and offered it to me with an attempt at nonchalance. The old major stood very close and nodded from time to time with what was intended for a pleasant smile. The lives of the garrison had been saved. Everything was going off splendidly. Alas, it was the lull before the storm. There is in every gathering of men one who is born to do the wrong thing. Some foolish Cretan, swelled with the conceit of ignorant patriotism, went up on the roof, pulled down the Turkish flag and replaced it with a Greek one. We on the inside did not know of this incident, but the admirals at Suda Bay knew. They did not intend to have their orders disobeyed and when they saw the Greek flag waving over the block-house they sent a messenger more persuasive than their first one. It came upon us unexpectedly and combined the qualities of an earthquake and a thunderbolt. I was afterwards told that it was a milinite shell from a French battleship. It struck the corner of the block-house and at the same time every nerve in the body of every man there. For my part, I could neither think nor move. I was vividly conscious, however, that every Turk who could get hold had a grip on my clothes and that the major was expostulating with me on account of this new calamity for which, in some strange way, he held me responsible.

The smoke cleared enough to show that no Cretans remained in the fort. With that perverse insistance on detail characteristic of a mind overcome by shock I noticed that the shell had cut the corner of the fort like a knife and that blue sky was visible through the smoke. All these events occupied only a few seconds of time; then thunderbolt succeeded thunderbolt. The minutes following cannot be described. The end of the world could not be more terrible than the concentrated fire of a large fleet on a lone block-house. Dust-laden smoke choked the air. Splinters flew, beams fell, pieces of wall caved in. A pandemonium of noise crashed in terror-giving dissonance.

How long it was before the idea that drives to action came I do not know, but of one accord we started to get out. The Turks still clung to my clothing. Forgetful of any obligation I was under to protect them, I vainly tried to get away. Together we ran stumbling through the smothering darkness for the door. We passed out of the fort while the shells were breaking in the wall above us. In the smoke we fell over some lifeless bodies, picked ourselves up and ran as we had never run before towards the mountains and safety.

By this time I had shaken off all the Turks except the major, who held fast to what was left of my coat. Curiously enough, he did not seem to delay my progress. On and on we ran, away from that hell, until the body could go no more. We stopped and looked back. A heavy concentration of smoke hid the ruins of the block-house. Occasional shells that missed the mark flew by, but these now seemed insignificant. Out of the cloud of smoke came what was left of the Turkish garrison, a sprinting line of blue uniforms. The humor of the situation brought relief. I laughed hysterically; the major nodded with disconsolate solemnity; the captain with the wound over his eye sat down and rolled a cigarette.

A Night at Death's Door.

When a man really makes up his mind that he will be dead within a few hours, living becomes a matter of very little importance. It is a fact that there is a strange calmness and lack of anxiety as a result of this condition of mind.

The experience which I am going to relate took place at Leech Lake, Minnesota, in October, 1898. I accompanied a company of United States soldiers to the Indian reservation and we were surrounded on a point of land forty miles from the agency. The little clearing in which the fighting took place was scarcely ten acres in extent. It was surrounded on three sides by heavy timber and underbrush, while on the fourth side was the lake.

The Indians were in the underbrush and although our little band of seventy soldiers had fought stubbornly all day and had lost nine killed, including Capt. Wilkinson who was in command, and fourteen severely wounded, they had been unable to dislodge the Indians.

There was a log hut, about twelve feet square, in the center of the clearing and at dusk we moved into that, while the soldiers dug trenches around it. During the night, which was bitterly cold, the soldiers were on duty in reliefs in the trenches, while the rest of us remained in the house. It is of that night that I am going to tell.

The log house, the abode of an old Indian, was dirty and ill smelling. We carried the bodies of the dead into the house and laid them in one corner. The wounded were placed in another corner and everything possible was done for them, but the lack of medicines and appliances made it impossible to assist them to any great extent.

After all had been done to make our position more secure and torem comfortable Gen. Bacon, commander of the department, who had accompanied the expedition as a spectator, Lieut. Ross, on whom the command devolved after the death of Capt. Wilkinson, three newspaper men and an old sergeant who had been in a score of Indian fights, held a conference. It was the most serious conference I ever took part in. The result of it was that all came solemnly to the conclusion that our usefulness, either as soldiers or correspondents, was at an end. We were evidently greatly outnumbered ; our men were nearly all raw recruits, the Indians were well hidden and could not be dislodged and, worst of all, our ammunition was almost gone. It was hundreds of miles to the nearest military post and help from there, at least help in time to be of any use to us, was out of the question. While we were discussing the chances of escape, a bullet came through the window, and after passing through Gen. Bacon's hat imbedded itself in the wall. That settled it.

It isn't often that men find themselves in a more desperate position. We could hold out but a few hours longer and when the Indians should make their attack at daybreak, as is their usual custom, escape would be impossible.

We didn't talk much after that—there wasn't anything to say. We stretched ourselves on the floor and thought. The hut was dark and cold. From one corner came the moans of a soldier shot through the body who was dying all too slowly. From the woods came the crash of the Winchesters, answered by the cracks of the Krags in the trenches. The bullets came like dull thuds against the log walls of the hut and every few minutes sounded the low, wierd yell of the Indians, the war whoop, than which there is no more hair-raising sound made by man or beast.

Every sound added to the assurance that we were as good as dead men. I made up my mind, as did the others, that it was only a matter of a few hours. But the worst thought of all was that we would be subjected to the horrible mutilations which we had all seen before, and which, having once seen, no man can forget. To be killed is one thing ; to have what is left of you hacked to pieces in the most horrible manner possible is quite another.

I was cold, tired, hungry and very thirsty and it was not long before nature came to the rescue. I went to sleep. When Lieut. Ross aroused me to tell me that dawn was approaching and that I had better take a gun and go into the trenches, I found that I was reposing comfortably with my head on a sergeant's knees and my feet on a brigadier general's chest. But they did not seem to worry about it.

Daylight came at last, but for an hour before there was no firing from the woods. The expected attack did not materialize; why, none of us have ever been able to discover. Had we been attacked we would, without doubt have all been killed, for there was less than 100 rounds of ammunition left for the entire party. During the day there was an occasional shot from the woods and one soldier who ventured out from cover was killed and another was wounded. Late that afternoon we were reinforced by a party of woodsmen who came by boat from the agency. A few days later the Indians came in, gave themselves up and the incident was closed.

But the events of that night in the old log house and the ring of those Indian yells will remain in my memory as long as memory lasts.

A Battle With the Waves.

As my experiences have not yet extended to the battlefield, this being my first war, I must perforce write of other than warlike matters, and have chosen for my narrative a battle for life in the surf on the coast of the Southern Pacific.

About the year 1889 or 1890 I was in Australia, living at a little seaside township near Sydney, on the shores of the beautiful harbour of Port Jackson. It is said to have been the place where Captain Cook first landed, and he gave the place its name of Manly Beach in honour of the manly spirit shewn by a black, who stood alone, like Horatius of old, to oppose the landing of the foreigners, when all his fellow braves had fled and hidden themselves in the bush.

The main part of this town stands on a narrow strip of land, only about a quarter of a mile wide, between the harbour and the ocean, joining the North Head of Port Jackson to the mainland extending round the opposite side of the harbour. I was in the habit of taking a morning dip daily in the surf on the ocean beach, and it was in the autumn of the year named above that my fondness for a bath nearly cost me my life.

There had been a tremendous storm which had stopped steamer traffic between us and Sydney, and had effectually prevented all bathing in the ocean surf, the waves being a sight only to be viewed from a safe distance. A few days later, when the sea seemed to have resumed its normal state, I thought I would re-commence my bathing; so with four boys who were under my care I sallied out to the beach about 6 a. m., and we took our plunge. As I had only lately recovered from a serious illness and was still rather weak, I soon came out of the water, and had dried and got on part of my clothes when I heard a cry: " V. is being carried out to sea!" V. was a youth of 17, nearly my own size, who I knew could only swim a few strokes, and sure enough was out of his depth, bobbing helplessly up and down, and every second drawn farther from the shore. I tore off my clothes and rushed in, feeling the water strike very chill as I entered it. In a few strokes I reached the youth and caught the hand held out to me. Then the struggle began. I felt the strong under-current as I turned shorewards, and my charge had no idea of raising himself flat on the surface of the waves, which would have impelled us shorewards, but hung his legs straight down and was pulled outwards by the under-tow.

By dint of hard struggling, and watching my time for each effort, I got him in a litttle nearer after some minutes' hard work ; but I felt my strength going with the cold and the fierce buffeting of the breakers, and knew I could not bear his weight much longer. Still we progressed, but as we got nearer shore the force of the under-tow increased, and suddenly a bigger wave than before broke right over us and the force of its impact parted us, V. being sucked under in the back-wash, and I carried forward on the crest of the wave.

I was just aware of the separation, and then I felt consciousness giving way. I looked up, saw dimly the roofs of the town which I felt I should never enter again, tried to give one last despairing stroke for self-preservation, and then knew no more till I found myself hurled on the beach and digging my hands in the sand. Once more I swooned, then another wave drove me higher up, and I lay I know not how long unconscious, till the voices of the other boys on shore aroused me and I struggled to my feet only to fall again a limp heap. Then my mind began to work, and I asked for V. "He has been carried out to sea and we can no longer see him." Can anyone picture the agony of that moment? Here was I safe on shore, and the youth committed to my care was drowned and his body carried out for the sharks to feast on. How could I ever face his parents and tell them the story? How could I ever explain the working of that dreaded under-tow? Would they not think I had failed in the hour of danger and left their son to his fate in order basely to save my own life ? Why had not I been drowned too ? Far better so than be alive and the boy dead.

Thoughts such as these crowded through my brain, when a shout came: "There he is!" It seemed my efforts had, after all, not been quite in vain. I had got him into an inner current and he had been carried down along the beach some 100 yards past us. There was hope, then, yet. What a revulsion of feeling! But what was to be done ? The three other boys stood helpless near me, stupefied. No one was in sight to help. I rose. I tried to run, but fell, being still too weak from the buffeting I had received. " Run, get ropes, get help!" I cried wildly in my despair. But houses were far off, and the boys only ran aimlessly along the beach—two of them, that is ; the eldest, a big, strapping youth of 17, taller than myself, stayed with me. "C.," said I to him, "you must go in with me and help me haul V. out." His only reply was that I was unfit to enter the water again. I knew it was a desperate expedient, as C. could not swim, and we might both perish without saving V. But it was the only chance; if we joined hands we might battle with the breakers and together haul him out.

We started off, but I fell two or three times, and I saw C.'s face quiver. He thought it madness, but went pluckily forward without a word. Suddenly appeared a man coming down to his dip, all unconscious of our trouble. I called on him for help, telling him our story briefly. "I cannot swim," he said, "we must send for other help." "It will be too late,"was my reply ; "we three will join hands, and together we can accomplish our purpose." He gave rather reluctant consent, and we made for V., who was now fairly close in, still bobbing helplessly up and down, but apparently still conscious. Our new-found friend now grasped the state of affairs, and was as keen as myself. He insisted on taking first place, I followed and C. brought up the rear. Firmly we clasped hands and entered the waves ; now we were near our half-drowned man, and in another moment our front man had grasped his arm near the shoulder with his disengaged hand. "Steady, all together, one, two, three," he roared, as a huge roller broke over us. I felt the strain, we staggered, but held firm, and with one more pull and a few steps shorewards we were in safety. We had conquered the waves and accomplished our task.

In a few minutes we had V. lying on the beach ; he had swallowed a good deal of water and had a nasty time of it, but had scarcely been out of his depth since I had given him my first tow shorewards, and in a few days he had recovered from his immersion. But it had been a close call for us both, and there had been more than one exciting moment in our struggle such as I do not particularly wish to experience again.

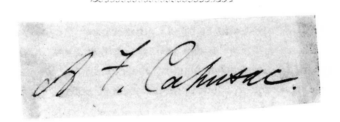

Michaels, of Michaelmas Bay.

To me this story has been interesting, for, in his way, Michaels carried his " message to Garcia."

We had been a month or so " on the job," as the saying was, (meaning the Spanish war), steaming from one West Indian port to another—the port depending upon how rival despatch boats were heading with the issue of the day's operations. We had to lay our course for the place where we could be sure of a clear wire to New York.

One story afternoon we saw the " Triton " trailing smoke in the direction of Port Antonio, and the " Corsair " making for Kingston, and the " Golden Brick " stealing up the Cuban coast to Guantanamo, and the lubberly " Three Friends "—she had a gait like a bear—pounding hard for Samana. All this meant that at these points cables would be occupied, and we would be shut out until every paper but ours had printed the story of the day.

" We might go to Panama," suggested Stephen Crane, " or "—with kindling imagination—" to Martinique."

" Haven't got the coal," said the Captain, measuring distances.

" There's Michaelmas Bay in Hayti ; can't you make that to-night ?"

" Never been up that way, and I don't seem to have the lights or soundings."

" Never mind," Crane put in, " We'll trust you not to ' collide ' with the island."

" There's a revolution starting in Hayti— "   " There always is," we interrupted.

Looking to see if we were serious, the skipper then turned, and rang " full steam ahead." He had a delicate taste for adventure himself.

Night fell black and furious ; and the seas played roughly with our little pilot boat from the Florida Keys; so that, writing in the cabin, an erratic pencil in one hand, we had to cling fast with the other to the edge of the table.

Finally we turned in, knees pressed against the side of the berth, to guard against being tossed out. Near midnight I felt myself pushed, pulled, and pounded, and heard Crane's voice calling: " Wake up ! Don't you want to see a ship climb a mountain ?"

On deck one got a strange impression. Close above was a deep purple sky, its gold stars seeming, for sleep-filled eyes, scarcely higher than the mastheads. The weather had cleared ; there was now that perfect tranquility which settles so often over southern latitudes. In the smooth water was reflected darkly and distinctly the mountain that backs the harbour of Michaelmas, and it did indeed appear that the ship's forefoot was on the ascent, moving up the steep Mole itself.

Anchor chains suddenly rattled, and the Captain jocularly called, as if he were docking a Coney Island steamer, " All ashore, who are going ashore." We dropped over side quite as we had come from our bunks, in pyjamas and yachting shoes, a little wad of money and a sheaf of telegrams in our handkerchief pockets. In place of the mirage, we now discerned ahead a level beach. All at once there flared up a row of crimson watch-fires. Odd human figures passed and repassed.

We had to wade ashore. The figures were in military costume— thirteen of them, every uniform ragged and different ; some from the Napoleonic era, some from the reign of George Third ; one had the tasselled helmet of the Kaiser's Hussars, several the fore-and-aft dress-hat of Admirals. All bore guns, and most were barefoot. The firelight showed them as black as the night itself.

They surrounded us, arrested us ; marched us up a muddy street. An abrupt order came to halt. Soldiers with torches were grouped about a long cannon, and we, as it happened, were alone in front of it, scarcely two feet from the muzzle.

Revolution in Hayti and we about to act in another Sepoy scene—

that was the first fleeting impression of this precarious situation.

"We're really not dressed for charades," protested Crane. "Stop the show and take us to the cable office."

We were carried on, and finally to the Governor's thatch-hut of a palace, where we were placed in chairs by a table covered with oilcloth such as you may see in New England farm kitchens.

There was a ladder leading to the attic. Sounds of scuffling, the ring of spurs on the floor above, and then a shining boot and a red trousered leg, and an embroidered coat tail, and a gilt sword, and at last heavy shoulders, epaulettes, cocked hat,—and the Governor had descended, back towards us.

His official suite, all black like himself, followed. They sat about as if upon a drum head court-martial, and heard the report.

The Governor asked: "Why do you invade my province at night?"

A light of understanding broke over his face when he heard that we were simply attempting to invade a cable office. "Ah, you know M'sieu Michaels?" he enquired.

"Yes, yes; our friend. But we'll see him in the morning. To-night we desire to go to the cable."

He reached into the pocket of the tail of his embroidered coat, and brought forth a pack of cards. He spread them upon the table with a sweep of the hand.

"Low deals," I suggested; and we, the prisoners, each drew one.

"No, no, Messieurs," protested the Governor.

It presently appeared that he wanted us to purchase the pack. Casually counting the cards we found there were only 51, but did not mention it, and offered some money. He pushed it back, "*Jambon*," he explained; "have you not American ham aboard ship? M'sieu Michaels, he say get ham."

"Michaels needs food?"

The poor chap was perhaps in hunger in this all but forsaken black place. "Take us to him. Yes, we have plenty ham."

Torches were relit; the guard led the way past scattered thatched huts, and up the stairs of the single two storey building, and opened a door. The moonlight showed three men stretched asleep. "Who is that?" came from one. At the reply, he leaped up and struck a light, and grasped our hands. It was Michaels. He was yellow, lean, haggard. There were two bottles of Vermouth di Torino on the washstand, besides an empty bottle marked "quinine," and an empty box marked "calomel."

"God, but you've taken your time about coming!" said Michaels. He began pouring out some vermouth.

"I did not ever really believe though that the office would let me die here."

We waited, uncomprehending.

"You can't help having hard thoughts you see, in a place like this— just a few huts on a hillside, only niggers around you,—except these two French cable operators, and the Governor's half white son,—and the whole settlement struck with yellow fever. Every morning when I get up"—he went to the casement and pointed—"I look out here, and I see one more poor body being borne in a wheelbarrow to a little raw hole they have dug in the hillside. It has got on my nerves. Medicine out; no ships coming in, food scarce, and my last $20, my last cent, went for that message to the Manager telling him he *must* send a boat for me or I'd be a goner. However, it's over. Here you are. I wish I had something better than vermouth to offer you, but it's good for the fever. You're Crane, are you? How long have you been with my paper?"

Crane was not with his paper; neither was I; and the one our boat belonged to was in fierce rivalry with that of Michaels. Now we were bound and pledged never to give transportation to correspondents of competing journals. We looked at each other. We explained that we were not the succorers he expected; that our boat was the *Planet's* boat.

Michaels' lips parted with something like misgiving; we could see his wretched depression returning.

"But we're going to give you a lift," we added; and his eyes lit up again. "Now wake your friends the telegraphers, and help us file our despatches."

The sleeping figures on the floor were rolled over and aroused.

They led us, the torch bearers accompanying, through brambles and cheparral to the little corrugated zinc cable-house solitary on a knoll — solitary in a place of solitude, yet in instant touch, through a wisp of wires from instruments on a side table, with the lovely human settlements of the world.

It was in instant touch ; but when Halifax was called upon to receive 800 words for New York, Halifax responded that it would not undertake anything so long at night. We would have to wait until the day shift of operators 6 hours later. We began to rage.

Thereupon Michaels said—"Leave your stuff with me. I can't go away with you, and I'll see that it is started at 8 in the morning." He thrust his hands in his pockets, then he pulled them out. The old frantic despondency was back.

"But, man, you're dying here breath by breath," we objected. "The place is torturing you into a hole in that hillside. You've got to come."

A look I've never seen before and that I can scarcely describe came over his face—the sort of look, I fancy, that Hubbard wore when his companions had to abandon him in the wilds of Labrador, with nothing left to subsist on but a pair of moccasins.

There was this difference. In Labrador the man was too weak from starvation to move farther ; at Michaelmas Bay the man was far gone with fret and nerves, and fever and loneliness ; he insisted on staying because his office had not itself released him.

He came out to the ship with us. We gave him ham, and we gave him potatoes and oranges and whisky. These we had to send ashore in a separate boat. All he asked for or would take himself, was a bag of North Carolina tobacco............

He did not die. When, after a despairing wait, he obtained

a transfer, and returned to New York, his office dismissed him. I don't know why except that it was some small matter of unnecessary expenses such as, I suppose, spending twenty dollars gold to ask for relief.

Franklin Clarkin

Fifteen Hours Under Fire.

This is the story of a day in the midst of a little war in the islands of a little people.

General Schwan with an expeditionary brigade was scorching his way down through the southern provinces of Luzon, encountering no pronounced shocks of battle, but a constant and irritating fire from remote hills and jungle shelters. I remember best of all the fourth day of the campaign ; and the recollections re-form themselves now much in the same words that made up my letter from the field.

The infantry outfits were emerging from a nightcamp at Binan, where an odor of gutter sewerage had mingled with the scent of roses. A mist of pearl and pink was wavering in the cool of morning over Laguna de Bay, and lifting from the hills beyond. From the head of the column there tumbled a series of commands, which halted the infantry and shoved it aside to allow Colonel Hayes and his Fourth Cavalry to take the lead. I butted my pony, a rag of a beast and a discard, in among the sharpshooters of the cavalry advance ; and one dusty trooper found occasion to remark that I would be toting my mount before night.

Mid forenoon, four hours afterward! A blistering highway which lost itself in brown, baking hills ; throats sticky from white dust and the air's scorch ; naked, imperious nerves from the unseen and unceasing fire! The troopers sat tight in the saddle, save the one or two in each outfit who carried no arms, clung to the manes of their mounts, and were held from lurching downward by the hands of their fellows.

A hundred yards ahead, a Filipino scurried like a rabbit across the trail, dragging his Remington, butt down. Ten feet to my right a carbine crashed. The native sprawled, shaking. We galloped forward. he steel from the Krag had entered the Filipino's chest. His face was turned upward. A lighted cigarette still adhered to his lips, and a bubble filled with the smoke of a last inhalation broke at the mouth of the wound as we watched. Someone laughed unnaturally. The words formed curses. No one claimed the shot.

Mid afternoon and scarcely a halt! The insurgents had deserted the foul, big town of Silang by the time we reached there. Every man prayed that the day's march was ended, but prayers availed not nor our dreams of coffee and bacon. Colonel Hayes did not even dismount at Silang and we had scarcely time to unbuckle a haversack before the trumpeter screamed " Forward!"

Between Silang and Indang there are fifteen ravines and as many ranges of rocky hills. We began the first ascent in a crushing pressure of afternoon heat. Meanwhile, I had dragged back to the fourth troop, and was bending under the curses of the cavalrymen because my staggering pony cluttered the way. There was a jam of men and horses in one of the ravines and it became necessary for the fourth troop to halt on a down grade. I remember that I was profiting by the interval to swab out the mouth of my pony, when a trooper standing just before me at the head of his mount, was struck to the trail. He had been holding a filled canteen in one hand. The bullet pierced the rim of the vessel and entered the man's abdomen. As his head sank forward it seemed that his eyes were fascinated by the water spurting from the hole in the canteen, which had dropped before him.

" L-o-ook at th-the b-b-lood run!" I heard him mutter.

Twilight in the mountains! The natives still dragging at the haunches of the column; the scream of a stricken horse; the grunt of a trooper, grazed or run through; the hoarse pantings of men and beasts, and the repeated yell of one officer, commanding upon the allied powers of God, man and the devil to " leave no wounded behind!"

The Colonel was a mile ahead in the mountains, and I was clinging to the last outfit now—Don Cameron's White Horse troop which had been ridden to the bone for days and could not keep up with the fresher portion of the regiment. In a stretch of level way ahead, I suddenly perceived a sorrel pony, placed there as if by divine dispensation. The tough and shapely little stallion was securely fastened by a heavy wire which ran from his neck into the jungle. Unable to cut or break the wire, I pushed back the undergrowth to seek the other end. Meanwhile, the last troopers were passing. I heard a rustle in the thick growth of bamboo, and an uncanny tremor passed coldly over me, I knew not why.

" Come out of there, you damn little fool! They're waitin' to carve you at the end of the wire! " yelled the last non-com in the column.

My tardy faculties grasped the ruse, and I scrambled onto the old pony in a severe state of thought.

Less than twenty minutes later, the White Horse troop heard a voice —a familiar-voice—cry out from the darkness behind :

" For Christ's sake—don't!"

A detachment spurred back and found a member of the troop prone upon the trail. His face and body was hacked. The bone handle of a bolo protruded from his mouth. The point was fixed in the ground, hammered by a stone through the base of the trooper's brain. He had halted in the darkness to re-cinch his mount, unnoticed by his outfit. As we rode away, there reached us from the jungle behind, a frenzied neighing from the captured horse—frenzied because of its separation from the troop.

Moonlight in the mountains, and the White Horse troop is miles behind. I do not know about the others, but I, on that torrid night, was shaking and chilled to the marrow from sheer fatigue. I had lost my spurs, and it is a harsh thing to think of now, but I kept the pony on his feet by stabbing his flanks with a leadpencil.

We reached a bridge about an hour before midnight and found that a part of the planking had been ripped away by the Filipinos. There remained for twelve feet over the gorge a stone girder seven inches wide stretching from the cliff to the solid planking. Cameron determined to force the horses over this girder in the treacherous moonlight. The first beast whirled screaming downward! The Captain spoke sharply to the un-horsed trooper, and made the second attempt himself. His own mount slipped and was lost—crashed down to a the rocky margin fifty feet below. Almost incredible is the fact that the other horses were led over in safety.

"I was never so humiliated in my life," Cameron whispered to me later, "and the ugliest sensation I ever encountered was when I let go Old Silver's bridle-rein."

Across the ravine the cavalry trails diverged. The Captain, not knowing which to take, ordered his men into camp after fifteen hours under fire. The harshest moment of that whole day to me was when coffee was forbidden a few minutes after the halt, because the necessary fires would draw shots. We rejoined the main body next morning at Indang which had been taken after a fight the evening before—but my pony—foundered—stayed behind at the Broken Bridge Camp.

"MY MOST INTERESTING EXPERIENCE."

PRESTIGE

The Dilemma of Another War Correspondent.
The Bear: "How shall I ever write it?"
By
Grant Wallace
"The Bulletin",
San Francisco. Cal.

My Most Strenuous Campaign.

On a stifling night in June, 1896, several men recently arrived from Washington sat on the steps of a Chicago hotel, discussing, as men from Washington invariably do, politics. One was Howard Thompson now engaged in telegraphing to the Associated Press from St. Petersburg official fabrications of the destruction of Japanese armadas. Another was a junior member of the junior house of Congress, an unassuming man clad in a linen "duster," whose face might have been that of a tragedian.

We were commenting upon the unprecedented lack of a presidential candidate for the Democratic convention which was to assemble on the morrow. Thompson remarked casually : "It's a dark horse. It might be you or I, Bryan." Everyone smiled, the politician in the linen duster with the others. Three days afterward we saw ten thousand people cheering for twenty crazy minutes the conclusion of his speech, " You shall not press this crown of thorns upon the brow of labor. You shall not crucify mankind upon a cross of gold." We knew that the silverites of the West had found their champion to free the Democracy from the domination of the Eastern gold bugs, and that the quiet man in the linen duster was the dark horse.

In July I received a telegram from the manager of the Associated Press : "Mr. Bryan will rest a week at Upper Red Hook. Join him and accompany him on his campaign tour."

After three exciting political conventions, rest at Red Hook was alluring. I arrived on a Sunday morning. Churchgoing is an important incident in the life under the calcium of a candidate and Mr. Bryan was to worship in the village church. Visions of the quiet little stone building and the soporific discourse of a country pastor promised a—peaceful hour.

"Some of the folks are comin' in from the country to see Bryan," said the driver who took me from the station. They did, some thousands of them. They filled the church and much of the park, surrounding it. Over the shoulders of the nearest stratum, through a window, with clothing badly damaged, I achieved six square inches of standing room in an aisle.

After church I must call upon the candidate to pay my respects. Most of the county were doing the same. Mr. Bryan shook the hands of voters and patted babies on the head, was jostled and trodden upon, and listened to the old platitudes throughout the long hot afternoon, while his host's garden was trampled into a wallow of mud, peanut shells and cigar stumps. Then, followed by a caravan of reporters, he drove five miles to a neighboring village to address a Sunday school gathering. Returning, we found the premises besieged by delegations from religious bodies who had come by special trains to obtain the views of the candidate upon " the alarming increase of the traffic in alcoholic liquors" and who afterward repaired to the hotel where the correspondents were stopping to enlist the power of the press in support of their crusade.

Monday's programme included two speeches in nearby towns, the reception of representatives of the Knights of Labor, Tariff Reform Leagues, Sons of the Silver States, Veterans of the Rebellion, Anti-poly-gamists, Anti-vivisectionists, Anti-lynchers, and Woman's Suffragists, always with an exchange of speeches; afterward a formal dinner with more speeches, and an evening made riotous by political clubs with torchlight parades and fireworks (more speeches), concluding with a serenade by the Lower Red Hook Silver Cornet Band.

Mr. Bryan was resting.

The first day of work he took a train, with his following of secretaries and reporters, did three large cities of central New York making eight speeches in halls and parks, and fifty informal talks at wayside towns, besides shaking hands with many thousand citizens. Instructions were to report the speeches fully. Panting stenographers and hysterical typewriters toiled far into the night. At every railroad station we thrust a huge batch of copy upon bewildered telegraphers accustomed to sending ten word messages. Each installment was headed "Add Bryan." Unhappily their arrival in the New York office was not in chronological sequence and that night of wrestling with "Add Bryan" is still a maddening memory with the editors. They continued coming in for a week and some have not arrived yet. At daybreak the correspondent was awakened to read a Napoleonic command, "Condense Bryan." The stenographers were already beginning to do so, for in such a flood of words there were naturally repetitions. One wriggle of the pencil represented "We can restore the free and unlimited coinage of gold and silver at the constitutional ratio of sixteen to one, without waiting for the aid or consent of any other nation on earth."

"Our Peerless Leader," as he was emblazoned by the transparencies, being "The Champion of the Plain People" could not accept the bribes of plutocratic corporations offered in the guise of palace cars. He rode in a plain passenger car and the plain people rode there with him. They purchased tickets to travel for the sight of a future president, and all the occupants of the train crowded into his car. The Oldest Inhabitant, the patriarch who voted for Jackson, the autograph stalker and the unknown genius who desired to lay a poem at the feet of greatness, clambered over our limbs and perched on our seats while we strove with pads on our knees to compose dispatches. The newspaper corps held no antipathy toward trusts. They accepted on the third day of suffering the private car of a railroad president and persuaded the candidate to ride there as their guest. Then an opera company playing "The Prodigal Father," with a fascinating chorus in straw colored hair, boarded the train. Since Our Peerless Leader was the Friend of the Working Man it seemed fitting that we should befriend the working girl, but when our other guests entered the car he betrayed his principles and withdrew from our society.

At Rochester twenty thousand Democrats heard their Peerless deal verbal body blows at the money power from a stand in the public square. Afterward he made a dash to catch his train, while the people surged after him to grasp his hand. Borne along with the current, my foot slipped on the wet grass. I awakened in a residence overlooking the park, with the fumes of ammonia in my nostrils and sympathetic ladies at the bedside, to learn that nineteen of the twenty thousand patriots had walked on my body. By that time Mr. Bryan had played engagements in seven towns. When I caught up with the expedition it was at Erie, State of Pennsylvania. The candidate made three addresses in three theatres that night and afterward the manager of the hotel which was least crowded provided blankets for seventeen journalists in a hall on the fourth floor. Mr. Bryan appeared on the balcony in response to the calls of the populace gathered in the street and spoke once more. By one in the morning the bands had played their last tune, the sky rockets had ceased to fizz, the torches had paled, the bonfires were burning low, and we thought the day's agony was done. But two o'clock came and excited voices were still wafted up to us through the night. Men were gathered on the sidewalk discussing the effect of the demonitization of silver on the price of wheat. The problem was one which confused eminent economists, but which the humblest Democrat in the land felt perfectly competent to expound. Anyone who declined to be convinced was in the pay of the Rothschilds and that ended the argument.

The representative of the New York Times, Irwin Thomas, like his brother the dramatist, had a rotund figure and clean shaven face. Gathering an ulster about his pajamas he stepped out on the fire escape.

"Friends and Fellow Citizens!" His voice rang out imperatively while he stretched a commanding arm toward the sky. "You can do it."

There was a wild cheer, followed by a hush, and all faces were turned expectantly upward to the speaker, as they thought, to the statesman from Nebraska.

"You can restore the free and unlimited coinage of gold and silver (cheers) at the constitutional ratio of sixteen to one without waiting for the aid or consent of any other nation on earth. (Tremendous cheers.) We have worked many days and nights to save this nation from the Rothschilds. We are tired. For Heaven's sake disperse, and let us have sleep."

Robert M. Collins

In Modoc.

" Lookout, Modoc County, California, five men lynched here last night. Particulars later."

That was the telegraphic despatch received in the San Francisco office of the Associated Press one afternoon in the spring of 1901 that resulted in an exciting experience in my career. Even in California news of sentence passed by Judge Lynch upon one man is of more than ordinary interest, and when the news came that the distinguished jurist had settled the fate of five men at one time, the wires were made hot with telegrams demanding the story. But the anxiously awaited particulars failed to arrive. The peaceful town of Lookout might just as well have been under the control of a Japanese censor for all the news that came from there. Lookout is only about 100 miles from the nearest railroad station, but a rather shaky telegraph line had been built into the country and there was no apparent reason for the failure to obtain the much desired " particulars."

The silence of Lookout became painful. When, a few days later, reports from Susanville, Amadee and Alturas stated that the law-abiding citizens of Modoc County had ended the careers of five of their number by dropping them off a bridge with ropes around their necks, there was a pardonable desire on the part of thousands of people in other sections of the country to know why. But the correspondents at Lookout, Susanville, Amadee and Alturas either could not or would not tell why, and it was up to me to find out.

I could not spare one of the office men, so I thought I would take a little run up to Alturas and ascertain what had been done. It is only a short journey of two and a half days by train and wagon from San Francisco to Alturas, and I needed rest. On the train I met a man who was a cattle buyer and who was on his way to Alturas. He became my guide, philoso-

pher and friend, and invited me to ride in his private conveyance from
Termo, the end of the railroad, to Alturas. It was a most uninteresting drive
through miles of alkali plains and sage brush. Hundreds of jack rabbits
and an occasional slinking coyote were all the living things we encountered.
As we approached Alturas an occasional ranch house gave indications that
the country was not destitute of population.

About two miles from Alturas my friend, the cattle buyer, halted his
team, handed the reins to me, and extracted a travelling bag from the bottom
of the wagon. He opened the bag and took therefrom two six shooters.
One was a revolver of large calibre, and the other a smaller weapon, but
apparently equally deadly at close range. After carefully examining the
mechanism of the weapons and loading them, he placed the large pistol in
a holster worn on a belt in plain view. The smaller weapon he placed in the
breast of a canvas jumper. I was an interested observer of these warlike
actions, and requested information as to their purport. Said my friend, the
cattle buyer :

" There's a fellow in Alturas who has sent me warning that he will
shoot me if I dare enter the town."

" Why don't you turn back ? " I inquired.

" I can't afford to," was the response. " If it became known that a man
could scare me away from any town by merely threatening to shoot me, my
occupation as a cattle buyer in this region would be gone."

" But why do you carry two guns ? " I asked.

" Oh," he said, " the big one is for show and the little one is for use.
You see, with the big gun in the holster I can talk to a man without making
a warlike move, as he will be watching my gun. If it comes to a show-
down, the little fellow in the breast of my jumper can be pulled before he
knows what is going to happen.

" But you need not be alarmed," he continued. " If there is going to
be a fight it will be a fair one ; he won't dare shoot me in the back, for he
knows what the people of Modoc County would do to him if he killed a
man in anything but a fair fight. It will be a question of who can draw the

quickest, and I reckon I can take care of myself. All you need to do is to keep your eyes open, and drop when the shooting begins."

We drove into Alturas and registered at the hotel. While we were waiting to be shown to our rooms we sat in wooden armchairs, our backs close to the wall, and facing the entrance to the bar-room. I was telling my friend some anecdote when suddenly, with hardly a perceptible movement of his lips, he said:

"Don't move; keep on talking; here comes my man."

I looked up, and saw in the doorway between the bar-room and the hotel office a tall, roughly dressed man. He saw us at the same time, gave a slight start, and then walked over to where we were sitting. The man's arms were hanging at his sides, and his hands were empty. I looked at my friend. He had not moved a muscle, and apparently was not even looking at the approaching man.

I tried to keep on with my story as instructed, but beyond a mechanical movement of the lips I doubt if I uttered a sound.

The big man walked from the bar-room, and as he approached, said:

"Hello, Burns! Are you 'heeled'?"

My friend nodded, and glanced down at the holster at his side. Instead of drawing a weapon, as I had anticipated, the big man extended his right hand and said: "That's good; but you won't need it. I want to tell you that I was mistaken about that matter. Will you shake?"

My friend, the cattle buyer, shook, and so did I, but in a different manner.

When we adjourned to the bar-room to indulge in the refreshment that etiquette in Modoc County demands upon such an occasion, the neck of the bottle played a lively tattoo on my glass as I poured out a drink.

I know that my fingers had made dents in the wooden arms of the chair where I had clutched them while waiting for the carnage to commence.

My nerves had not recovered their normal condition that evening when three residents of Modoc knocked at the door of my room, and were admitted. They inquired my business in Modoc County, and when told that I was travelling merely for pleasure and for rest, they informed me that the climate of Alturas was very unhealthy for strangers, and out of friendly interest in my welfare, they would advise me to return to San Francisco. I had no desire to leave Alturas, but their arguments seemed most convincing, when my friend, the cattle buyer, came to the rescue. I was introduced to my three visitors as his friend, and they were told that I was all right.

I remained in Alturas a few days while the grand jury was busy indicting the principal citizens of the county for participation in the lynching of the five men, and was allowed through the courtesy of the committee to telegraph the story to San Francisco. An old man named Clark, his three half-breed Indian sons, and a hired man had been gently suspended from a bridge at Lookout one night. They had been guilty of horse stealing, cutting harness and hamstringing valuable animals for motives of revenge.

The men who were indicted for the lynching were acquitted after a short trial. The lynching was an expensive administration of justice for the good citizens of Modoc County. An extra tax for the expenses of the trial was levied upon them, while at the same time they were contributing liberally and privately to a fund for the defense of the alleged lynchers.

How Stephen Crane Took Juana Dias.

At the close of the Spanish-American campaign, the American forces that landed in Porto Rico, were supposed to be invading a hostile territory. Politically, as a colony of the enemy, the inhabitants of the island should have been hostile, but they were not. They received our troops with one hand open and the other presenting either a bouquet, or a bottle. Our troops clasped both hands. There still remained in many of the towns a Spanish garrison, but from the greater number these garrisons had been withdrawn upon San Juana. As a result scouts and officers of our army on reconnaisance were constantly being welcomed by the natives as conquering heroes, and at the approach of one of them, entire villages would capitulate as readily as though the man had come leading an army corps. One town surrendered to an officer who had lost his way, and stumbled into it by mistake, another fell to the boss of a pack train, whose only object in approaching it had been to steal some ponies.

In order to make quite sure, some towns surrendered several times. Ponce for instance surrendered four times to as many different American officers. It was not safe for an American wearing anything that resembled a uniform to approach a Porto Rican stronghold unless he was prepared to have it fall prostrate at his feet.

It struck me that in this surrendering habit of the Porto Ricans there lay a chance for great entertainment, and much personal glory, especially as one would write the story oneself. It would be a fine thing I thought to accept the surrender of a town. Few war correspondents had ever done so. It was an honour usually reserved for Major Generals in their extreme old age.

Half way between Ponce and Coamo there is a town called Juana Dias which, at that time, seemed ripe for surrendering and I accordingly proposed to Stephen Crane, that at sunrise, before the army could advance to attack it we should dodge our own sentries, and take it ourselves. Crane was charmed with the idea, and it was arranged that on the morrow our combined forces should descend upon the unsuspecting village of Juana Dias. We tossed to see who should wake the other, and I won the toss. But I lost the town. For in an evil moment Crane confided the strategy of our campaign to the manager of his paper, the New York World, Charlie Michaelsom, and Michaelsom saw no reason why in this effort to enlarge our country's boundaries, a man representing a rival newspaper, should take any part. So, no one woke me, and while I slumbered, Crane crept forward between our advance posts, and fell upon the doomed garrison. He approached Juana Dias in a hollow square, smoking a cigarette. His khaki suit, slouched hat and leggings were all that was needed to drive the first man he saw, or rather, the man who first saw him, back upon the town in disorderly retreat. The man aroused the village and ten minutes later the Alcade, endeavoring to still maintain a certain pride of manner in the eyes of his townspeople, and yet one not so proud as to displease the American conqueror surrendered to him the keys of the cartel. Crane told me that no General in the moment of victory had ever acted in a more generous manner. He shot no one against a wall, looted no churches, levied no "forced loans." Instead, he lined up the male members of the community in the plaza, and organized a joint celebration of conquerors and conquered. He separated the men into two classes, roughly divided between "good fellows" and "suspects." Anyone of whose appearance Crane did not approve, anyone whose necktie even did not suit his fancy, was listed as a "suspect." The "good fellows" he graciously permitted to act as his hosts and bodyguard. The others he ordered to their homes. From the barred windows they looked out with envy upon the feast of brotherly love that overflowed from the plaza into the by streets, and lashed itself into a frenzied carnival of rejoicing. It was a long night, and it will be long remembered in Juana Dias. For from that night dates an aristocracy. It is founded on the fact that in the eyes of the conquering American while some were chosen, many were found wanting. To this day in Juana Dias, the hardest rock you can fling at a man is the word "suspect." But the "good fellows" are still the "first families."

In the cold grey dawn of the morning as Crane sat over his coffee in front of the solitary cafe, surrounded by as many of his bodyguard as were able be about, he saw approaching along the military road from Ponce a solitary American soldier. The man balanced his rifle alertly at the "ready," and was dodging with the skill of an experienced scout from one side to the other of the long white highway. In a moment he was followed by a "point" of five men, who crept close to the bushes, and concealed their advance by the aid of the sheltering palms. Behind them cautiously came the advance guard, and then boldly the Colonel himself on horseback and 800 men of his regiment. For six hours he had been creeping forward stealthily in order to take Juana Dias by surprise.

His astonishment at the sight of Crane was sincere. His pleasure was no less great. He knew that it did not fall to the lot of every Colonel to have his victories immortalised by the genius who wrote the Red Badge of Courage.

" I am glad to see you," he cried eagerly, "have you been marching with my men ? "

Crane shook his head.

" I am sorry," said the Colonel, " I should like you to have seen us take this town."

" THIS town ! " said Crane in polite embarassment. " I'm really very sorry, Colonel, but I took this town myself before breakfast yesterday morning "

"He that Died o' Wednesday."

"Honor is a mere scutcheon."—*Sir John Falstaff*.

All his life the Major had been only "the son of his father." Boyhood, youth and early manhood he spent basking in the sunshine of the older man's greatness. Wealth and social position were his without thought. There was no need to strive.

The father died and he became head of the family. Then came the war. When his regiment arrived in Manila, men said it was the powerful influence of his mother that had secured his commission, and the proud will of his wife that had caused him to accept it. He was to prove himself worthy to bear his distinguished name.

He possessed in large measure the common heritage of his race, simple courage. The time soon came to show it. It was his first action. His battalion had the advance, and the Major marched not far from the point. From an ambush beside the road came the sudden bullet that struck down the sergeant in the lead. As the man fell the Major sprang forward and caught him.

"Get a surgeon!" he shouted.

The nearest man turned to obey. As he started a second bullet speeding from the ambush stretched the Major on the ground, his arms still round the man he had tried to help. The column swept by up the road and the fight was on.

Three days later I was standing on the Mole in Manila, in front of the Depot Quartermaster's warehouse. Down the street a slow procession came, led by a solemn band playing its ever recurring Chopin march. Overhead not a cloud flecked the blue. Soft sunlight filled all the squalid place. The air was as balmy as on a warm spring day at home.

About and inside the warehouse men were hard at work, Filipinos and Chinese coolies, half clad, ragged, dirty, sweating under huge loads, pushing boxes, hauling bundles, rolling barrels. In the midst of the turmoil they set up two trestles. There they placed the casket, covered with the bright, beautiful flag he had served so briefly.

Ranged on each side were the men of the funeral party, bare headed. Outside, the unmoved, long practised band waited to play the quickstep. By the head of the casket stood the Chaplain, thin, wan, fever-stricken. Three or four women leaned against the wall by the doorway, furtively wiping their eyes. One unreservedly buried her face in her hands and sobbed. The Chaplain lifted a thin hand, the color of the faded khaki of his uniform :

" I am the Resurrection and the Life," he began.

The Filipinos and Chinese outside wrangled about their work or shouted at one another in rough jest. A passing tug screamed shrill warning to a pull-boat in the river.

" Man that is born of a woman," solemnly repeated the Chaplain, " hath but a short time to live and is full of misery."

A line of four-mule wagons came lumbering down the Mole, pounding noisily over the rough pavement, the drivers angrily calling to coolies to get out of the way, demanding their freight, quarrelling with one another and their lot.

"Earth to earth," said the Chaplain, slowly, "ashes to ashes ; dust to dust ! "

The trumpeter grasped his bugle and stepped to the foot of the casket. Slowly, softly, the notes of beautiful " Taps " floated through the throbbing warehouse, and for the moment hushed the noise of toil and strife. Outside, men instinctively stopped and uncovered, the last tribute of the brave to the brave.

The bugle ceased. The men lifted the casket and carried it to the launch that was to take it to the transport for its journey home. The band struck up its quickstep and marched away. The "son of his father" was mustered out.

Oscar King Davis.

One Day's Work in Cuba.

There are thrills and thrills in the life of every war correspondent, and I am tempted to indulge in introspective analysis of my feelings when attempting to select that commanding moment where my climax of human emotion was reached.

I find moments when horror has overcome me, when fear has paralyzed me, when poignant grief has constricted my heart, when sympathy and pity have deeply stirred my soul, when humor has shaken me with laughter, and pathos has bowed my head in tears, and when all or many of these have combined to hold me bound in awe at the destruction produced by the passions of men swayed by a common impulse and cause.

As an illustration of what I mean, let me take the campaign in Cuba, alone, where a sensational engagement of a day, off the harbor of Santiago, and one fierce battle on land, before that city, resulted in the capitulation of the Spanish army and the signing of the protocol.

I stood by Grimes' Battery in the early morning of July 1st, 1898, while the gunners with deliberate care threw shell and shrapnel at a Spanish block-house far in the distance. A small army of eager-eyed correspondents crowded around the battery, interspersed with a galaxy of foreign military and naval attachés, immaculate from the waist-line up in full-dress uniforms, and bedraggled and mud-bespattered, as regards their nether garments. A sort of festive occasion, a premature bit of Fourth of July celebration, if you like, with bursting shell replacing paper wads !

Some two hundred yards behind the battery stood El Poso house, with its white stuccoed walls and curved red-tiled roof. A small clearing separated the house from the impenetrable tropical forest, with its dark-shadowed trees festooned with sinuous llanias, and an underlying jungle of cruel, sharp-spiked Spanish dagger plants and cacti. Here several thousand

soldiers were basking in the gratifying warmth of an early morning sun,
and, after the chilly night advance, thawing out their cold-benumbed
frames.

Six shells screamed from the guns, growling, droning, and finally
sighing away into the purple-tinted vista of palm-crowned hills. Then
the earthquake came : The purple distance had thrown back the devilish,
screeching shells. One—two—three—four—five—six—they came, almost
as I slowly count them, and, with the accuracy of previously well-platted
range, they fell on the guns of our battery, one shell actually bursting on a
gun and killing and wounding four artillerists, another tearing off a cavalry-
man's leg not twenty feet from where I stood, a third crashing through the
red-roofed house, and others dropping in the very midst of the reclining,
closely-clustered Rough Riders and Third Cavalrymen.

Presto! Change! Up the nearby hill the plumaged attachés fled,
outrun by nimble war correspondents, leaving the artillerists grimly to
serve their guns alone. Unfortunately I had a horse—acquired by strategy
and retained by the simple process of daubing out the branded U. S. on his
flank with yellow mud, and filling the deep-cut numbers in his hoof with a
similar clayey preparation—and I did not feel inclined to desert him in his
hour of need, so I retreated on foot, leading the startled animal by the
bridle-strap, toward the main highway connecting Santiago with the coast.
As I ran, our Cuban allies, in their white cotton clothes, fled with me,
throwing themselves prostrate on the ground as each shell roared over our
heads, or bursting pieces hurtled cruelly near our ears.

A dazed moment of relief, at finding myself outside the concentrated
zone of fire, in the narrow main trail congested from forest wall to wall with
troops, and then the military balloon came sailing around a corner, a hundred feet above the tallest trees, and into plain view from the Spanish position, whereupon their artillery fire was promptly directed upon it.

Five minutes with Grimes' Battery and then ten minutes of hell under
the military balloon, as I vainly yelled "Gangway" from my saddle, and
pleaded with soldiers who, with eyes strained skyward, were ducking
shattered shrapnel, to let me advance! I could not go rearward, as the

troops were moving forward and had the roadway solidly packed.

Perhaps this was my most interesting fifteen minutes!

An hour later, I lay behind a five-foot embankment at the "bloody angle," vainly trying to regain control of a rattled heart, personally safe, but horrorstruck at the sight of men dropping, wounded or dead, faster than I could count them, as they rushed through the waters of the little brook, in plain sight of the Spanish block-house six hundred yards away. During a lull in the advance over the stream, a lone soldier came into view, sprinting fast, doubled up with his head below his waist-line and gun swinging at arm's length near the ground. When he reached the muddy bank of the brook, his feet apparently slipped, and he plunged head first into the water. A laugh went up, but was hushed as suddenly when the gentle current turned upward a dead face, with a bullet-hole in the white forehead, and a pennant of red blood rippled with the waters of the shallow stream. Fifteen minutes, and a hundred lay dead, dying or wounded under the shelter of the bank, brought from a radius of only thirty yards.

Was my climax of emotion reached here?

Sixty minutes after, and I lay alone, far to the left of the bloody angle, flat upon my face in a grass-grown road, with ten inches of protecting earth in front. The Sixth Infantry had cut the lower wires of the bordering fence and six hundred men had crawled away on all fours, into the waist-high grass of the open field directly in front of the block-house perched high on San Juan hill.

The roar of small arms, rapid-fire guns and a limited amount of artillery pelted the ears with racking vibrations, and, from the bushes a few feet overhead, leaves and twigs cut by bullets dropped in a continual shower. The frenzied horror of the child, aroused from slumber and lost in the dark of its own comfortable room, the childish terror of a dark night in wind-swept woods, peopled with monsters of the imagination, do not equal the sensations of a timid man lost in the conflict of battle, without sight of human being, touch of flesh, or word of mouth to give him courage.

Through a small opening in the intervening shrubbery I could see the block-house; minutes seemed to drag into hours, as I lay prone upon my face, with eyes just peeping above the earthen bulwark. Then across my field of vision, only a hundred yards away, strode General Hawkins, hip-deep in the tangled grass. Over his gray head, which shone as silver in the sunlight, he swung his campaign hat, while behind him marched a bugler with swollen cheeks, blowing the charge, only the faint echo of which reached me above the din. A straggling line of men rose, one by one, above the yellow swaying grass-tops, and plunged stumblingly forward for San Juan hill.

A revulsion of feeling, from abject terror to maddening patriotism, swept me to my feet, howling and cheering fiercely the men who so bravely stormed the hill, and then, with a realizing sense of personal danger, I once more clung to earth.

Was this my fifteen minutes, or was it that night on the battlefield, when a full and brilliant tropical moon encompassed the hill and valley and forest in a pure white light, and the stillness of the night, without the quiver of a leaf, seemed, in comparison with the noise and thunder and fierce struggle of the past sun-scorched day, like the silence and softness of eternity? The high grass of the now silent field of death had changed to a sea of silver, and, from its shallow depths, cold, white-faced men peacefully stared into the beautiful heaven beyond, content at last.

My bunky was dead; the companion, the chum, the friend with whom I had shared the pleasures and difficulties of long preparation for the campaign, until we had learned all of one another's little secrets, failures, successes and ambitions in life. "Sorry, old chap. Yes, he's been killed. Brave soldier. I don't know where he is," they told me, with a clasp of the hand and a glisten of the eye.

It was like a dream, some story I had previously read, so unreal and yet so real, as I wandered over that battlefield alone, looking for my dead, and I felt not only my own grief, but the grief of mothers and wives and sisters and sweethearts, who, with strained and quivering nerves, were waiting in far distant homes for the blow that would sadden the rest of their lives.

There lay a soldier, with his face to the moonlight, and eyes closed so softly as to make it hard to believe him dead; here someone had kindly placed his campaign hat over the staring eyes of another, that he might sleep, and yonder another lay prone upon his face, with his rifle beneath him, still fiercely gripped in his hand, and there and there, the silver sea was strewn with them ; and at last I found my bunky—not sacrificed in the dead level of the field below, for he had climbed the hill, in the fearful joy of the combat, to the very edge of the Spanish trenches themselves.

As I took away from him all his little trinkets and personal effects, to send to the sister whom he supported at home, the words of his good-bye that morning rang incessantly in my ears: " Bunky, I'll come out of this a colonel or a corpse," and the refrain ran, over and over, " A corpse, a corpse, a corpse."

Was this my fifteen minutes? I leave it to you.

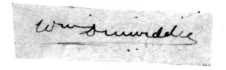

A Startling Surprise.

It was in April, 1900. The dark days of the early South African campaign were now numbered among the events of a nation's history and Lord Roberts at the head of a magnificent army was sweeping towards Pretoria. I attached myself to the cavalry paving the way for the onward movement that was intended to envelop the principal towns of the Transvaal.

One morning after a dusty march beneath a scorching sun we sighted, far across the bare, brown veldt, the town of Kroonstad. Together with the correspondent of the "Times" I rode forward with the cavalry patrol despatched to reconnoitre what was regarded as a vitally strategic position. After fording the river a hard, fast gallop brought us to the entrance to the town. The main body of the enemy had retired some time before our arrival and the local authorities under the circumstances deemed immediate surrender advisable. Not a single shot was fired and beyond a sinister expression of sullen regard from the people lounging about the streets, there were no evidences of hostility, real or implied. Soon afterwards the patrol withdrew from the town to rejoin the main body of the army, the "Times" correspondent and myself remaining behind. When the town became deprived of armed authority, the Kaffir population, whose love for their former masters, the Boers, was not particularly striking, ran riot in the market place fighting, with all the fury of savage instinct let loose. We endeavoured to quell the disturbance by riding our horses through and through the mob. The "Times" correspondent inspired a good deal of respect with a revolver which he carried, but unfortunately I was armed with nothing more formidable than an ordinary hunting crop.

When something like order had been restored, I left my colleague, who had firmly mastered the situation, and went for a Four round the town. In view of the complete and ready surrender I unhesitatingly ventured here, there and everywhere, without fear of meeting an enemy. But I soon received a startling surprise. Riding past a low stone wall which surrounded a pleasant little villa, I espied a vision that made me pause with a rapidity that might be taken for shock. Confronting me was the black barrel of a rifle pointed straight at my head by a black-bearded Boer. It was certainly a moment for prompt action. Within the space of about a minute I explained to him that the town had unconditionally surrendered, and added, with an originality and quickness of thought that since has often made me marvel, that the British troops were in possession and that an vast army was close at hand. Almost simultaneously there popped over the stone wall nineteen more bearded faces and nineteen more rifles. I realised my danger, but with an assumed air of unconcern I informed the "opposing force" that as their position was hopeless they must immediately lay down their arms. Happily for me, they followed this counsel. When I entered the enclosure beyond the garden wall I saw that each man carried a plentiful supply of ammunition and learnt that the chief of the contingent was the noted Wessels. Without a moment's delay they handed over their rifles with a child-like faith in the veracity of the receiver which at the time I thoroughly admired. The "bag" also included twenty horses and equipment. I stacked the rifles on the inside of the wall and ordered the men into the street. Still I did not feel that the incident was satisfactorily closed. Twenty men in charge of one man armed with a hunting crop certainly held the balance of power. For two hours I mounted guard over the prisoners. It was perhaps the most uncomfortable two hours I have ever spent. Occasionally the prisoners becoming curious, would ask leading questions, the answers to which called for some inventive skill. But I spoke in stern tones and did my utmost to look the part I was playing. Great indeed was my relief when I saw the figure of a horseman galloping towards me. Presently a life guardsman reined up before the villa and I related to him that the twenty men sitting in a row were prisoners of war, adding that I would require his services to assist in maintaining guard. With much significant display he drew back the bolt of his rifle, and placing a cartridge in the barrel pressed it home with an emphasis that was not lost upon the group. Now the prisoners appeared to realise, more acutely than before, that the army had actually arrived and at last I breathed with the freedom of a man who was no longer a prisoner of his prisoners. The clatter of galloping hoofs heralded the approach of mounted troops, and when they had entered the town, we two, the life guardsman and myself, escorted our contigent to the Provost Marshall. Kroonstad had been captured and twenty prisoners.

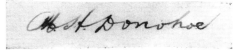

The Penalty of War Corresponding.

Through the nebulous mists hanging in thick, clammy folds over the Eastern Sea but a month ago shot the piercing, opalescent rays of a far-reaching flashlight. Horizontally, perpendicularly, obliquely, the light clove the nether dark of the night like the ghost of a great knife. Now it hesitated as some fishing junk came within its focus, and anon it trembled as a lesser object rose upon the swelling sea. Presently it stopped suddenly in a sweep of the wave surface and settled penetratingly upon a steamer surging its way eastwards to Japan. Upon her white upper works and masts the light shone phosphorescently and limned her out against the crowding darkness like a phantom craft. Passengers on her decks wore spectral faces, and but for the rapid beating of hearts which came upon the ears like the monotonous rapping of temple drums, it would have been difficult to tell that they were living beings. Clinging to the pendulous rails, which rose and fell with rhythmic motion, they peered at the spot where the brilliant rays converged, hoping by some supernatural agency to have the nationality of the vessel staring at them displayed to their view. All around and beyond the glaring disc was dark as despair. Nothing but the noises of the night—those creaky, ghostly sounds which invest a ship afloat on the lonely ocean—could be heard. Everything was oppressive, uncanny.

All that could be seen was the flashing of the near wave crests and the nearer spindrift flying in blinding sheets from the cut water. Closer and closer crawled the light, faster and faster sped the steamer to avoid it. An apprehension of approaching danger possessed all on the ship, and fears were shared even by those in precipient positions. Stokers and engineers toiled with the energy of despair in the grimy, feverish stokehole, and on the deck the Captain and officers paced nervously, delivering their orders in monotones scarcely audible. Swish! Almost with a noise, as the blade of light swept through the air from sight, the world was plunged in utter darkness deeper than the gloom of Stygia. Eyes could not see farther than the rail for what seemed an hour, but when sight was restored a vision which struck terror into every heart appeared. Not more than a quarter of a mile away was a huge cruiser looming up like a great black monster. From her sharp steel stem water spouted in miniature Niagaras. Behind her trailed fast turning masses of smoke. Her speed was " full ahead," her intent; to cut us down. With a roaring, crashing, blood-curdling tumult she clove like a flying thing through the resistless waves. Men of stout heart trembled. Their blood ran chill through their veins. Their hair moved with that strange creepy sensation that unusual fright produces. " Man the lifeboats! man the lifeboats!" The order came in terrible tones from the bridge. There was a wild rush of men; a clattering ring of the telegraph to the engine room; a sudden, violent, soul-stirring shudder, and the vessel swept midst surging commotion in the sea upon a backward course. " Hard a port!" yelled the Captain, with eyes glued upon the advancing mass of steel. " Hard a port, it is," answered the voice of the helmsman. The vessel appeared to scarcely respond. " Hard a port, I said!" roared the Captain. " Hard a port it is," murmured the helmsman. In horror men almost lost their wits. Onward with thundrous noise sprang the mighty ship. Her forward guns, her anchors and chains, her bridge and masts, became plainly visible. She was a Russian—and cleared for action. Slowly astern and to port swung our apparently doomed vessel. But a hundred yards separated us, when, with what looked like a gigantic leap, the cruiser rose in the air.

Men shut their eyes and clung to whatever support was near. The roar of waters, the screech of steam, the uproarious rattle of racing screws, combined to drown all other sounds. With hearts in mouths and limbs limp with fear men held on, waiting for the end. There was a loud Russian howl of disappointment, a rocking of the steamer, a roar of a passing ship. Away across our bows the cruiser shot like a rocket. Men found their voices and cheered. " Boom!" The cheers were drowned in the wild, mad screeching of flying shells. The battleship went astern, her starboard swung round, and from wreaths of white smoke poured a deadly hail of shell. Masts and bridge and rigging were ripped asunder and toppled on the decks like limbs lopped from trees. The moans of dying men filled the air, and the shout of the men at the wheel aft that the rudder had been shot away showed survivors that chance of escape was gone, that resistance was useless. Slowly the cruiser swung round and drew nearer. Voices of men on her deck could be heard. Above all was the gruff roar of the commander on her bridge.

"Potopit sudno," (sink the ship) he cried again and again, but so great was the excitement that no one heeded him. Men crowded along the bulwarks waiting with grappling irons in hand, and as the ships crashed in an embrace the command " Gotovsya k pristupu " (prepare to board) was obeyed instantly. Tough, villainous-visaged men clambered to the rail. With victorious shouts they leapt to our decks and rushed upon passengers and crew wherever they could find them, seized them and bound them.

" Vzyat vsyeh v plen," (make everyone prisoners) shrieked the commander as he clambered to our "focsle" head. His order was useless, for all were tied with rope by this time and paraded on the deck. Dirty, ill-kempt Chinese stokers stood shuddering beside men dressed in the latest fashion of the Strand, and to these a Russian Lieutenant in broken English addressed himself.

" Ize sorry," he said, " but why you no stop ?"

" We are English! We stop for no man when there's a chance of getting away," answered an engineer.

" Ah, so! Your ship, what iz it ? "

" The Hyphun."

"Ah, ha! Ze newspaper ship—zese are ze correspondents ! " he shouted in glee, pointing to half a dozen men tied up near the companion way. And a demoniacal smile spread over his face as he interpreted the information to the commander. For a second or two the two engaged in a hasty conversation.

" Kajdi k borta," (tie every man to the rails) shouted the commander, in Russian, and promptly each person was seized, shoved to the ship's rails, and there lashed up.

" Zese men of ze papers write ze bad story of ze Russians," the Lieutenant sneered meaningly, as he pointed with his sword at the correspondents, who were now tied hand and foot facing a firing squad which had been ordered from the cruiser. " Zey must pay ze penalty."

An order in Russian caused a scurry of half a dozen men to the cruiser, and presently they appeared with armfuls of the newspapers published throughout the world. The Times elbowed Collier's Weekly. The Standard struggled for breathing place with Australian dailies. Out of a corner poked the head of the Chicago Tribune, and in desperate grapple were the New York Herald, the Daily Express, the Chronicle, and the Daily Mail. The London Daily Telegraph endeavoured to spread itself over the combined papers of the Associated Press. The mass looked grim. Every one wondered what was next. Russians grinned at each other as the commander and his officers conversed with one another. Suddenly the Lieutenant turned to the correspondents:

" Ze first of ze punishment iz this : Each of ze correspondents pick ze papers of hes office out, and each stand up wid hes paper and read what he hesself has written."

A bland smile, despite the seriousness of the situation, overspread the countenances of everyone. All the correspondents were untied, and reluctantly the papers which each represented were picked from the pile. They were a sorry lot who faced the Russian commander, but the majority smiled and blessed themselves that they were not connected with the Associated Press. Cold winds tore through the wreckage of the steamer, and with the aid of a flare light the correspondents read their writings aloud. The punishment was great. At the conclusion, all were once again bound up to the rail.

"Zat will teach you," uttered the Lieutenant between his teeth, " not to write ze story of ze Russians. You will have ze opportunity now to write ze last time."

As he moved away, men approached carrying bowls and open clasp knives. The correspondents began to say their last words; but the end was not yet.

" In ze blood from each," spoke the Lieutenant, " you will write ze apology."

Indignation flashed from every eye. Without a word being spoken it could be seen that there would be no apology. Each correspondent was approached by a Russian holding an open knife. A second man held a bowl. The man with the knife rolled up the left sleeve of his particular victim and despite the straining to break the bonds which the correspondents put forth, an incision was made, and from it spurted a stream of blood which was neatly caught in the bowl. Sharp-pointed sticks and a sheet of paper were then placed in front of each man. The right arm of each was released and the command was issued to write. No one budged. Again and again the Lieutenant ordered the pens to be taken up. Not a move was made. He became exasperated.

" Men of ze guard," he cried out, " form up !"

Twelve of the marines, armed with rifles, stepped up and stood ten paces from the bound men.

" Tree minutes,"—screeched the Lieutenant, " and you no write ze apology, I will fire. One,—Two,—Present ze arms—

" Tree,—Fire ! " Twelve streaks of livid flame leapt from twelve rifles. I felt a stinging sensation on the left side of my head. I fell—and awoke.

My head had struck against a trunk in a cabin of the steamer Empire then tossing and tumbling in a gale off Nagasaki. I pinched and shook myself to see if I had been dreaming. I had. The sun of the 7th of February was streaming in through the port hole. The crockery was rattling a feu de joie in the pantry.

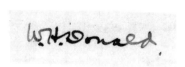

Arrival of the first Japanese soldiers at the gate of Pyng Yang.

Photo by Robert L. Dunn, Collier's Weekly.

February 8th.

On the momentous night of Febr. 8th, 1904, I was representing *Collier's Weekly* in Chemulpo, Korea. The cold was intense. In my heavy ulster I carried a magnesium flash lamp and all its paraphernalia. Being the only photographer in that part of the country, and realising the value of the unprecedented opportunity, I had for two weeks been working with jerky haste to and from Seoul, twenty-five miles away.

We were waiting in suspense for tidings from Tokio or Petersburg, but had learned nothing of the state of diplomatic negotiations. There was much suppressed excitement, everyone felt that war was certain. For days the harbor of Chemulpo was studded with foreign fighting ships.

About nine o'clock a light flared at the entrance to the harbor. Another and another and still another came, until what appeared to be fifteen gigantic fireflies were seen bobbing on the water. As they came closer to shore, we realised that these lights signalled the coming of Japanese transports. Everyone in town crowded to the water's edge to meet them.

For light to land their three thousand soldiers the Japanese seemed to have filled pails with burning oil which they tossed upon the water. These flickering lights proved to be huge torches in the hands of soldiers coming ashore in launches. Along the shore large bonfires were lit and frequently saturated with oil. Intersecting the log fires, huge iron tripods were erected with suspended pots of charcoal. This varied illumination gave the town a brightness like daylight, and could be seen for miles. It threw a fantastic halo in the heavens and was intense enough to make fine print legible.

While coming ashore many troops were frost-bitten. Seeing the fires, they scrambled for a place around them. Some leaped waist deep into the icy water, so eager were they for the expected comfort. They were, however, soon called to order and marched shivering to the adjoining street, there to await the coming of their fellow soldiers. The excitement was at its height and the troops, in absolute silence, were hugging the log fires, when a cry went up :

" The Russians !"

It came from the townspeople who had been frightened at the flash of my lamp as I took a picture of the scene.

The Russians were crowding, shoulder to shoulder, the decks of their men-of-war, from which they saw the passing of the transports and the first landing of Japanese troops in Korea. None realised that within twenty hours many of them would be torn to pieces by an accurate rain of shot and shell from the hidden Japanese fleet which then lay just outside the harbor.

Few people, if any, slept that night, nor the following night. The Japanese had come, had safely landed; " what next?" was heard from every lip. Wishing to see the meeting between the Japanese and Korean soldiers at Seoul, the capital, I hastened there by the first train. The picture was alive with war. I felt that the inevitable clash was on. Soldiers were arriving, entering the gates, passing through the city, and lines of Japanese school children were massed in different sections to greet them Following the soldiers I went to the barracks to get a photograph of the great tiffin which was to be served there at noon. At the spoke of twelve I asked an officer for permission to make the picture. As I spoke, a dull boom smote my ear and the officer thrust the crossed forefingers of his left hand into my face as he raised his right to his ear. In Japanese-English he exclaimed :

" Russian-Japan-cross-hear-hear."

As he shook the tightly clenched fingers of his left hand in my face, I heard cannon again, again and yet again. The guns were booming in quick succession, the first guns of the war, twenty-five miles away at Chemulpo.

The officer's word was sufficient ; I forgot the mess.

Leaping into a jinriksha, I yelled to the kuruma that he could have five yen if he could get me to the railway station in ten minutes. He called two men to help him and the three earned the money. But there was no train. All schedules had been broken by the movement of troops. Yet there was a mere chance of seeing the battle which I could plainly hear—how madly anxious I was to see it may be imagined!—if I could get to the San Do station, seven miles away, for the trains from Chemulpo might come that far and return immediately.

My kurumas were tired out. I got another, then another, and inside of three blocks had secured five more, until I had seven madly hurrying me through the village, over frozen rivers, through heavily ice-crusted rice fields, and, worst of all, the great sand plains. I rode, then I walked, then ran, perhaps I swore. F. A. McKenzie of the *London Daily Mail* was accompanying me, but in the sand plains I lost him. Later I saw him on the train, and knew that he, like myself, had overcome many difficulties.

A thousand dollars could not charter a train at San Do, not even an engine. Had I been a Japanese, all would have been well. Being a foreigner, even with money, there was no help for it but to wait for the regular train. In five minutes I discovered that looking at my watch retarded the movement of the hands. At last came the train. We scrambled on board, McKenzie and myself. It was slow, disgustingly slow. But we got there.

Once in Chemulpo, I ran to the water's edge where there had been hundreds of sampans. Now there were none. The Korean ' sampanners ' had taken to the hills. By persuasion with gold and a club I eventually got four. The tide was on the turn, flooding strongly. It was hard for my heavily-manned sampan to get to the U. S. gunboat Vicksburg. On the way out, I crossed the sizzling waters over the exploded wreck of the Russian cruiser Koreetz. I clambed up the side of the Vicksburg and found no one to welcome me or stop me from boarding. All were watching the actions of the defeated fleet.

The Varyag, powerful as she had been only a few hours since, rolled with every wave of the incoming tide. Her funnels were perforated, half of them had been completely torn away. Her decks were strewn with wreckage. Every gun was twisted and almost completely dismantled; coats, caps, boots, here and there a stray decoration, were flung across deck plates already dyed with blood. Small lights appeared almost simultaneously over the ship. They flickered, flamed, then flared into a huge torch.

On every foreign ship the bridges and decks were crowded by those who knew that forty-two dead bodies were being cremated in that livid heat. The fire seemed to have broken out in the exact spot where the bodies had been hurriedly placed by the fleeing Russians. As the sun sank, a huge torch rose, its flames leaping higher to prolong the day artificially. As darkness approached—a darkness which none noticed and few comprehended—the Varyag tottered and leaned heavily to Port. As she listed the flames grew.

In the midst of this gigantic bonfire, held in the broad harbor of a neutral nation, with men of many races for spectators, came the music of the holacaust—the detonations of exploding munitions. The magazine was afire, and for long minutes we watched the burning of a seven million dollar American-built warship. No one could lift a hand. With each move of the Varyag, hundreds of eyes were cast at timepieces; each spurt of flame, each detonation, each list, were accurately timed. Then came a cry, " See the Sungari !—She's aflame !" From starboard to port rushed every man on the Vicksburg to see the second bonfire.

Then we saw a ghastly thing. A boat left the Sungari and in its wake the flames spread from the steamer's prow to stem. The man in the rowboat had fired her deliberately.

Now the Sungari added her pyramid of light to that of the Varyag. On every other ship men rushed from side to side, dazed, not knowing what they did, calling to others, " Look, see her burn." About six o'clock, the Varyag's rail touched the water, then her funnels, then—she disappeared.

The Sungari burned to the water's edge. She sank as the day rose.

The Cowboy and the Rattlesnake.

I would write of a large rattlesnake, a great, lumbering, half-waked boy, an early morning, and a change of careers. I was the overgrown youth and it was the rattlesnake that gave me the thrill of my life and converted a discouraged young cowboy into an indifferent reporter. In my early youth my thoughts and hopes ran not to the sea and piracy but to the plains of the Great West. It was of the wild, free life of the cowboy that I dreamed, and when in fancy I saw myself I was astride of a noble horse sweeping across the prairie. I wanted to kill an Indian or two and was not averse to closing with bears. I made a lariat of the family clothes-line and practised on the dog and cat. The dog grew unfriendly and the cat abandoning the yard became fond of the roof. I stealthily acquired a revolver and spent hours perfecting myself in a quick "draw." My indulgent but wise parents watched the growth and development of this ambition with complete unconcern and just when I had completed plans for running away they told me quietly that I might go and be a cowboy all I liked.

Ten days later the casual observer passing through the Salinas valley in Southern California might have seen a very sunburned, very sore, very subdued young cowboy mounted on a muchly pinto-ed pony following in the dusty wake of a band of extremely tame cows. The Indians had long since passed to their happy hunting ground, the bears were dead or hibernating, and gone were most of the illusions of the life that in fancy had been so picturesque. The country was parched by a succession of droughts and lay barren and desolate under the white sun. My brother cowboys did not aid my falling enthusiasm for the wild, free life. I was generally required to rise first, eat last, and do the unpleasant chores. When we were bringing cattle in from the hills that extend like capes into the valley of the Salinas I it was who rode to the ridges, and when we were driving the sorry beasts along the shallow, shifting stream that is called the Salinas I it was who rode in the center where the quicksand beds were numerous.

In my lonesomeness I tried to make friends with my ugly pinto horse, but he was not be trusted ; he was deceitful. He could buck beautifully, kick quickly and gracefully, and bite firmly with all of his teeth. He would lead a decent life for a time and just when I began to suspect that he had reformed he would artistically demonstrate that he had not. His gait was not exactly the poetry of motion and when we jogged along we generally failed to jog at the same instant. He bucked and shook much of the waning ambition out of me and prepared the way for the coming of the snake.

The day-to-day routine of ranch life was finally broken by the rodeo or round-up. We had to pick out several hundred beef cattle for the market, and brand the yearlings—a task that required days of planning and preparation, an extra force of men, and much hard work for everyone. A good round-up is worth while. We used no corrals, but held the cattle on the plain in a great band. The segregation of the beef cattle was easy, it was the branding and ear-marking of the yearlings that furnished the excitement and fun. Among undomesticated cattle this is the yearling's first touch of civilization and if he takes his medicine easy he is distinctly an exception. We worked in gangs, part mounted, part dismounted. The first mounted man threw for the forelegs with his long noosed rope, and when he had made good, the second mounted man threw for the hindlegs. When both lariats were fast the riders started in opposite directions and Mr. Yearling was quickly extended on the ground. Some of the fights were great and generally after an hour's work the entire band was in a state of stampede constantly.

The rattlesnake came on the morning of the second day of the rodeo. At the close of the first day I turned in dog tired and passed away as soon as the blankets were tucked around me. It was not sleep, it was a trance. Next I knew, some unwelcome hand shook me and a voice said : "Kid, the foreman's hankering for you." Sleep-sodden and unwilling, I crawled out and donned my cowboy uniform. A flickering candle lit up the bunkhouse. It was 4 o'clock and still stone dark. I found the foreman working by the light of a huge bonfire near the stable. He was repairing a saddle and when I appeared he said sharply: "Kid, there's a stirrup in a soap box under one of them bunks in there. Git it."

Still partly under the spell of the night's trance, I ambled back to the bunkhouse, fished around in the dark for the soap box, found it, and then dug around in the box for the stirrup. The small, flat box was filled with various odds and ends and my hand located everything except the article I wanted. I finally decided to take the box out to the fire and picking it up started out. I had hold of either end of the box with my thumbs downward on the inside. One thumb encountered something soft, round, and flexible. It gave under the pressure of my thumb and I concluded that the box numbered a piece of rubber hose among its contents. As I reached the fire I leaned forward to place the box on the ground. There was a sharp rattle and then something came up out of that box and struck at my face. I cried in terror and jumped backward just in time to avoid a poisonous blow. My piece of rubber hose was a great rattlesnake angry at the intrusion of my hand and keen for another blow at me. He hardly reached the ground before he coiled for another spring. Just as he coiled, the foreman, cool, courageous and resourceful, reached him with a short stick and deftly tossed him into the blazing fire. He made one last, desperate attempt to raise his head, but by the flight of a second the fire was master. I came back to the fire and silently watched my enemy burn. The foreman was the first to speak. "Kid," he said and he measured his words with the deliberation of a judge, " you city guys is damn fools."

I went the rodeo through, but five days later the station agent at Bradley, Monterey county, sold one first class ticket to a city called San Francisco and the conductor on the up train that day punched the ticket.

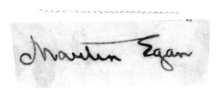

How South Americans Fight.

It was my good fortune—or misfortune according to the point of view—to take a hand two or three years ago in one of the little border wars that spring up periodically between South American States, when they don't happen to be in the throes of a revolution. I went as a correspondent; I stayed as a soldier; I returned as an invalid.

There is a prevalent impression in North America and Europe that South American wars are opera bouffe affairs, the scenario and plots of which depend on a comical combination of a minimum of fight with a maximum of flight. The dramatis personæ are supposed to be the defaulting president of a republic, scheming senoritas, loyal Anglo-Saxon adventurers, an angry mob of bedizened admirals and generals without followers, and an occasional poor super of a soldier or a peon with nothing but a thinking part.

Such, at least, were my impressions and anticipations of South American warfare when I first went down there. What rather puzzled me at the time was why the newspaper that sent me did not prefer a cartoonist. Perhaps the loss of a cartoonist would be taken more seriously.

Had I but clung to my preconceived notions I might yet have emerged from South America as a literary humorist. As it turned out, I took so sympathetic an interest in the domestic infelicities of the belligerent parties that I soon became useless as a correspondent, but all the more eligible as a combatant.

The truth is, nobody feels much concern about the wars of South Americans except themselves. The only way to stimulate a personal interest in their affairs is to become one of themselves. The full force of this was borne in upon me one time when I had crossed the Sierra Nevada of the Andes and had paddled over two hundred miles of inundation to get to the nearest cable station. There I received this message from my original newspaper sponsor: "Don't cable more battles. Nobody cares who wins." It was about this time that war correspondence in South America began to pall on me.

Seen at sympathetic close range, South American war is distressing to a degree. As you take in all the miseries and suffering it entails on thousands of poor people who have nothing to do with the making of war you also come to perceive the utter wickedness and folly that lies at its inception.

A battle which costs the lives of several thousand harmless country people, who have been dragged into the war very much against their will, may be opera bouffe to newspaper readers in another country, but to the mother and children of the slain it is very grim reality.

The worst sufferers, invariably, are those who have least to do with the war,—the women, the children, the aged and helpless, and the foreign traders. Yet, such are the soldierly virtues of these people that the very men who have nothing to gain and everything to lose, stand their ground the most manfully when it comes to a question of life and death. Even the starving women at home shrink from letting a foreigner suspect the full measure of their distress.

War in South America, such as I saw it at least, is unrelieved by any of the amenities of modern warfare. Few, or no surgeons accompany the troops, and there is no ambulance corps. So far from having ambulances, they have not even stretchers. The wounded are suffered to lie where they fall, until their comrades can look out for them. Mortal gangrene is one of the commonest sequels of a wound. The nearest hospital is mostly several days, journey distant. Even if there were ambulances they could not be moved, as there are no roads to speak of. Hence, there is a minimum of artillery, and that mostly of the lightest mountain calibre. As like as not the ammunition will not be forthcoming at the moment of action.

I remember one French artillery officer who commanded a battery of mountain guns in the Andes. When I came across him he was serving his guns without a range finder. He told me he had lost his glass at the beginning of the war and had not been able to find another. He was very loth to waste his ammunition at long range, and at one time had to be put under arrest by our commanding general for refusing to search the enemy's position with his projectiles. Inasmuch as his supply of ammunition was limited, there was some show of reason for his insubordination.

The common soldiers, in South America, are not so economical. They fire whenever their officers let them, without ever sighting their rifles. Only a few raise their gun barrels to a level with their eyes. The favorite method of firing is in volleys, the men squatting down with their rifles lifted barely to the middle of their bodies. Naturally almost all the long range fire goes high.

When the enemy is engaged, firing only becomes generally effectual at the near range of four hundred yards. Then it is deadly. But the issues of battles are still decided in South America by storming tactics and hand to hand fighting. Even in the face of machine guns, or against a well directed fire from behind stone walls, South American soldiers will charge straight up to the enemy's line with a reckless disregard of life that suggests hysteria.

I had a peculiar experience of my own with a machine gun, as handled in South America. While in transit from Panama to Venezuela, when our ship touched at Savanilla, I watched them tranship a Maxim from our steamer to their railroad cars. The men who were in charge of the gun stupidly left behind all the ammunition that went with it. At the last minute, when we were already warping from the dock, I drew the attention of our Captain to this. Then there was great excitement, and the boxes were lowered in haste and sent ashore in a boat.

Several months afterward I found myself on the desert peninsula Goajira leading a detachment of Venezuelan soldiers in a fierce ambush fight against the Colombians. During the fight, which was presently turned into a rout for us, a solitary machine gun gave us much trouble. Two infantry assaults were tried on it with disastrous results. Finally I was dispatched with a remnant of cavalry to take it from the rear. Screened by a hill and trees we succeeded in doing this. The gun was taken with a sudden rush and the briefest of hand to hand fights. It was the same gun that I had seen unloaded at Savanilla, and for which I myself, as it were, had furnished the ammunition. The gun was captured too late to do us any good. When the flight came I could not get her across our flimsy hanging bridge over a mountain torrent. We had to throw the gun into the water. Incidentally we also had to leave behind all our horses and pack train. The bridge was cut down only in the nick of time. Our heaviest loss in killed and wounded had been during the infantry assaults on the machine gun. The poor fellows had charged up within fifty feet of the gun.

The elite troops of South American armies are still the macheteros, the men with the machete, who give the turning point to a battle, as did the swordsmen of old. The wounds that are inflicted with the machete, which is nothing but a cane knife shaped like a European butcher's cleaver, are ghastly to look upon. Another favorite weapon is the pistol, mostly an American or English built revolver, but this is only carried by officers. Spaniards and Latin-Americans are very fond of mother-of-pearl handles for their swords and pistols, but they rarely carry more ammunition than ten cartridges.

While in the field, officers and men have the utmost latitude in their uniforms and accoutrements. One man will wear the heavy broadcloth of the regular parade uniform, with heavy boots and cork helmet, while the next in line will have a straw hat with pyjamas and sandals. I recall the General of a division riding into action in an undershirt and the lightest of sandals on his bare feet. His aide-de-camp, on the other hand, was attired like a Cavalier trooper, with huge boots coming over his knees, an ivory hilted Toledo blade hanging from a silken sash, a mother-of-pearl handled pistol and silver spurs.

Prisoners of quality are still held for ransom, while common soldiers who are taken prisoners of war are simply enrolled in the ranks of the captors. The fact is that the belligerents on both sides are so like each other in looks, in speech and in uniform that there is sometimes no distinguishing feature but the flags. Some of these, even, are disconcertingly alike.

The only time that I recall when the national flags of both belligerents were used, was when a column of eleven thousand Colombian regulars moved from Cucuta across the border upon the strong Venezuelan hill-town San Cristobal, where they knew Uribe-Uribe with his rebel refugees lay hidden. The town, perched high in the hills as it is, with only steep, zigzag mule paths approaching it, was considered impregnable. When Cipriano Castro made his famous march from Cucuta to Caracas he was careful to skirt around San Cristobal. This time, however, the Colombians thought they could take San Cristobal by surprise. In truth they came very near succeeding. It was only the desperate rally of Uribe-Uribe and his Colombians, who, having all at stake, flung themselves into an exposed church yard in front of the Venezuelans, that saved the town. The road commanded by this church yard, behind the perforated walls of which Uribe made his stand, ran up to it with a double zigzag at an elevation of nearly twenty-two degrees. Having failed to surprise the place, it was the sheerest folly of the Colombians to attempt a frontal attack on such a position. Yet this is what they did,—not once or twice but half a dozen times. They lost over eighteen hundred men. In the end the Venezuelans brought a plunging artillery fire to bear and, meeting the repulse with a counter charge down the steep slope, drove the Colombians off in pellmell flight. Had Uribe-Uribe followed this up with a strong pursuit he might have realised his long-cherished ambition to capture Cucuta and the rich valley around it.

Such is war in South America. As the Europeans settlers are fond of saying: It is all very well for the Americans to claim that the Monroe Doctrine has saved South America from Europe, but is there not need of a stronger, more forcible doctrine that will save the South Americans from themselves.

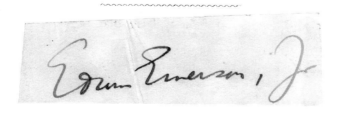

The Hat and the Ha'penny.

The penny is a luck piece, but the hat stood incidentally for a piece of luck. The penny hangs on my watch-chain and is one of the two superstitions that are left me, the other being the Star of Theodore Roosevelt. The hat was not my own, and is not now, but I wore it once in the Kentucky mountains, looking for the owner with another purpose than to restore. He lost it through a bullet, but came near getting it in the same way, as well as the head under it, which was mine.

The penny came from the hand of a Kentucky girl on the day I left for the war in Cuba, and to this day she does not know its story. I had no superstition then, but I took it as I would have cheerfully taken poison from such a hand, and I put it in my pocket and carried it for the sake of the hand, not for the power of the penny. I was at Caney in the morning, the bloody ford and San Juan in the afternoon, and I had one or two rather narrow calls—so narrow, indeed, that to the penny I straightway began to pin my faith. One day I was stretched out with fever, and that same day the penny was gone. That meant that all was over with me, and I meant that I would lay my bones in the shade of no sheltering palm, but with my fathers under the blue grass sod of Old Kentuck. I escaped form the hospital, got aboard a troop-ship, painted my yellow tongue red when held up in quarantine at Tampa, went delirious and unremembering to the chief city of the Commonwealth, and was picked up walking the streets on a hot August day with a temperature—mine—of 106. Some weeks later I got out of a hospital alive—alive, of course, because that good penny was not lost, but came back again.

Of the thousands of men who passed along the San Juan trail the day I found it missing, the one of the three soldiers whom I knew in the whole army picked it up near where he saw me lying last. Apparently he carried it for months as a luck piece himself. Christmas drew near. Probably, thinking of his wife and children and friends, he was led in this way to think that the penny might be somebody else's luck piece and perhaps mine. On this many-thousandth chance he sent it where he thought it might be sent on to me. This is simply theory. All I know is that on the following Christmas morning, a penny dropped out of a soldier's letter postmarked Vermont and that it was mine.

The hat is another story, as Mr. Kipling, I am sorry to say, has not observed for several years.

I was a member once of a volunteer police guard in the mountains of Virginia, a guard that had to take the law into its own hands, and from the law never strayed a hair's breadth. We had hanged Talton Hall, we had hanged the Red Fox of the Mountains, and we were now after the Fleming Brothers—Cal and Heenan—outlaws. The law-abiding natives, emulating our example, were helping us and hearing that they were likely to capture them, I had gone off on my own responsibility to the Pound, forty miles away, to join them. Mounted on a gray mule, dressed in the blue serge and broad-brimmed straw hat of civilization, I joined them about four o'clock that afternoon in the search. There were with me, Doc Swindall, Ed Hall, Goose-necked John Branham, so called for the length of his neck, and several other mountaineers. As we started out one of the mountaineers looked at my straw hat.

" Hell !" he said, " they can see that hat o' yours a mile through the woods. I'll git ye a hat."

He went inside his cabin and brought out a faded, shapeless piece of headgear, and I put it on.

When we were half a mile out in the woods he turned with a grin :

" That's Heenan's," he said, and the others laughed.

Both the outlaws were hiding wounded in the woods, and the dog, gun and hat of one had been captured that morning ; so I was wearing Heenan's hat looking for Heenan.

For two days we searched bushes, ravines, swam the river back and forth, tracking those outlaws through the woods, nor would it have been a healthy piece of business had we found them, as they could, of course, hear us coming and would get in the first fire.

On the third day we split up into squads. Swindall, Goose-necked John Branham and two others were under me, and that morning, luck was mine. At one spot in the woods the path forked, one trail going up a spur and the other around a side of the mountain, and we stopped there to decide which path it was better to take. At that moment the outlaws were lying in a thick clump of bushes twenty yards above us, wounded and with their Winchesters cocked and aimed, waiting for us to take the path up towards them. I had never seen Heenan and he had never seen me. But he knew his hat, and he had it most carefully covered with the sights on his Winchester, and the head under it, as well.

The rest wanted to go up the spur, but I decided, with no reason then, and no reason that I can think of now, to take the other path around the mountain side.

The two lay wounded in a cave for two weeks, Cal Fleming letting ice-cold water drop from the roof of the cavern on a frightful wound in his breast, until both were well enough to escape in women's clothes into West Virginia. There they were captured by Ed Hall, Doc Swindall and Goose-necked John Branham. Cal Fleming was instantly killed by Hall. At the same moment Heenan shot Hall through the back of the head, dropping him to his knees. He wheeled, stretched Branham out on the floor with a bullet through each lung, and Swindall with a bullet through his neck.

That left the duel between Heenan and Hall, who, with a lucky shot, blew Heenan's pistol from his hand. Heenan fled into a back room, and finding no egress, came back to the door with his bloody hand aloft.

" Well, Ed," he said quietly, " I can't do no more. I give up."

I had left Heenan's hat in the mountains. Two months later I saw him in the court room, thin and pale, and with the scar of a bullet on his chin, being tried for his life, and I walked up to him. I thought he would surely be hanged, but if he wasn't I wanted to be as friendly with him as possible.

"Heenan," I said, "did you ever get your hat back?"

Heenan grinned.

" No," he said,

" Well, if you come clear, go up to Dotson's store, get the best hat you can find and have it charged to me."

Now, through the death of the witness on whose testimony his accomplice, the Red Fox, had been hanged, Heenan actually did come clear. And the last I heard of him he was riding out of town on a mule with his baby in front of him, and on his head a brand new derby hat—mine. The exchange was apparently satisfactory, for Heenan never took the trouble to look me up again, nor have I ever sought very vigorously to meet him.

Two months later I was telling this story at a luncheon at a New York club and my mail was brought in just as I finished. In it was a verification of the tale—a bill for Heenan's new hat.

A Night Attack on Boshof.

It was a chilly experience, even for Africa. It took place at Boshof, in the Orange River Colony, on November 22nd, 1901, during the Boer war. I was with my regiment, the 4th Scottish Rifles (the Cameronians). Colonel Courtenay (afterwards C. B.) was commandant of the garrison. We were waiting for orders to advance towards Hopstadt and Kroonstadt. Troops were scattered all over the town, even the churchyard being commandeered to house them. They were cuddling under their canvas seeking shelter from a downpour of rain.

My company was stationed at the main entrance to Boshof, together with G company, under Captain Lynch. We were hourly expecting another attack, and were dying for another good brush with our worthy foes.

Not far from where we were stationed was a stream which flowed around the town. It fed a large reservoir which the Dutchmen had built years ago as a bath, but it had been little used for some time before we occupied Boshof, for the Dutchman who took pleasure in a bath had seemingly passed on.

It was a bright moonlight night. The croaking of the frogs was the only sound which reached our ears, for this reservoir was full of these noisy jumpers. Other than the frogs' chorus we heard nothing but the occasional lowing of oxen or the growl of a regimental pup and the occasional challenge of the sentries.

I suggested a swim in the reservoir to Captain Melville. He at once approved. We stripped and left our clothes in a corrugated iron hut close by, which a Kaffir had built for the use of the troops when bathing. I plunged in and upon coming to the surface heard " the last post " being sounded. The last notes had barely died away before a fusillade was opened by the Boers.   A shower of bullets fell spluttering into the water all around us, chipping off pieces of the stonework of the reservoir.   The pick-pock of the Mausers could be heard on all sides.   Bullets were whizzing all about from a range of about a thousand yards.   We lost no time in scrambling out.   Capt. Melville reached the steps first.   He was struck in the buttock by a bullet and fell back again into the water, but soon recovered and crawled out.

It was useless for us to think of reaching the shanty where our clothes were, for the lead was rattling against its side like popping corn in a grid. We were in a position that was far from pleasant, but had to do something, so we dashed in our nakedness towards our men.   Poor old Melville was bleeding from an opened wound, but he insisted that he was all right.   He shouted to me ! " I'm all right Glossy : I'm as right as rain."

He was running along twenty yards to my left, and the bullets were singing.   There was an uproar.   From all sides we could hear the sound of galloping artillery, batteries dashing along the streets to their positions at full gallop.   Bugles were sounding, rifles cracking, and alarm after alarm was sounding all over the place as company after company got into action.   As you can imagine, I was excited, and reached the trench wearing nothing but a broad smile ; in fact, I will not even vouch for the smile, for I think I was too scared to muster one.

Naked, I took charge of my men in the trench.   The Boers tried to press home their attack at the north end of the town.   At our side of the town—the East—their fire though troublesome was intermittent.   Three hours afterwards we learned that the enemy's attack had failed, thanks to the skilful handling of the garrison by Colonel Courtenay.

You have no idea how cold it can get in Africa in the early morning, and I shivered as we went from trench to trench while the engagement lasted.   And as for the Tommies, I was no small source of amusement to them as I ran about like Adam, but without the proverbial fig leaf.

Finally, when the enemy drew off, I borrowed my sergeant's coat ; and cuddling up in it I rolled over in a trench and slept in my position ready for a renewal of the attack which never came.

When I awoke the sun was shining and things were quiet. Later, I went back to the bathing—place to get my clothes, but they were perforated all too much to be of any further use to me, and I congratulated myself that I was not in them when they were perforated. Had I been, I should not have been privileged to tell you this story.

With Colonel Yankoff: A Balkan Episode.

Like the hollow of a giant's hand, the valley lay girt round with hills, great hills that rose majestic in their solemn splendour ; flanked with black pines and covered with wondrous wreaths of snow, grim, gaunt and grey they stood like sentinels of time, watching the footsteps of the passing years—God's outposts amidst the wilderness of trees. Upon the topmost height the sunlight caught the snow, gilding the fleecy mantle with the soft sweet flush of dawn. In the cup of the valley the untrodden carpet lay just as it fell from the Maker's hands, white, stainless, echoless and still. No patch of brightness to relieve the sight but that pink halo riding high around the very brows of the rude crag that frowned unceasingly upon the world, all else was passionless ; dull black, or white as winter. No sight or sound of life, no tinkle of the herdsman's bell, no lowing cattle, no bleat of sheep, no woman's voice, no maiden's song, no strong man's cheery laugh, no baby prattle, only a ruined hamlet, roofless, fire-scarred, and stained with richer dyes than red wine leaves on boards of pine, with here and there a dead man lying on the ravished threshold of a home ; for the shadow of the Turk was on the valley of Mujitje, and all the land of Macedonia wept for woman's wrongs.

Five days before, I had looked upon that hamlet smiling to the skies, a little patch of peace, untouched, unsoiled, by war. Then, children played before the cottage doors, and granddames sat within the shadows of the walls weaving with old, deft fingers the linen none should live to wear. Then, men, strong in their mountain strength, carried the fodder from the hills to feed the stalled cattle to fatten for the markets in the spring, and peace, white winged, lay like a benediction on the Christian valley. Then came the Turk and after him came this. The maidens were upon their way to Turkish harems, the old folk or the little children were either dead or wandering homeless and famine stricken in the bitter mountain fastnesses and Yankoff and his band were looking down upon the scene with eyes heavy with the lust of vengeance.

Yankoff, half mountaineer, half Viking, was the greatest fighter whom I ever looked upon, great in his physical strength, great in his lionlike courage, great in his love of home and country, great in his purity of soul, great in the volume of his hate for the foes of his country's freedom. He stood there a towering, frowning figure, his immense black beard blown by the morning's breeze across his chest, his carbine clenched between hands that had grown from boyhood around weapons of war ; gentle as a matron by the camp fire, tender as any girl to a wounded comrade, kindly and forgiving to a manly foe in the hour of that foe's defeat, but a devil hot hoofed to the assassin, and the ravisher. As I looked into his face a great awe came upon me, for I knew that I was looking into the face of retribution. The eyes that had twinkled into mine full of mirth a few hours before, were hard as an eagle's now; the mouth that had smiled so readily in welcome when I asked to be allowed to attach myself to his band had grown like a cleft in a granite boulder ; the flush on his dark, strong face was like the flush from the half-opened lid of hell. He turned and spoke a few words to his men, and they, because they were weary with forced marching, threw themselves down under the pines and rested. But even as he rested every man's hand played with his yataghan, and every eye was turned upon the chief, and every eye asked eloquently for vengeance.—An hour passed by, and then out of a narrow pass that led into the valley opposite where we bivouacked came a band of Turkish marauders, not the regular soldiery of the Sultan, but Bashi Bazouks, fierce, untamed free lances who hated all the Christian world and would slay for the sake of slaying. With a wave of his arm and a low, exultant shout, Yankoff brought his men to his side. They crowded round him like hounds round a hunter, watching the foe file into the ravine below. They saw him throw his carbine down with the low, rumbling laugh that they knew so well, saw him toss back the sleeve of his mighty right arm, until the white flesh and the big muscles lay bare, saw him draw his big, curved sabre from its sheath with an upward and outward sweep of his arm, and then they knew that the hour they longed for had come, and each man bared his steel.

Then came a sound like the soughing of the sea, a sound like the rush of wind through swaying trees, a sound like a ripping gale when the spume of the ocean is tossed amidst the shingle of the coast, and Yankoff and his band were rushing down the mountain's side like a torrent down its bed. They paused not, halted not. Leaping over fallen trees, bounding over clefts and chasms, they flung themselves upon the foe, and drove right through them as lions drive through deer. Then steel met steel, and yell answered yell.

Chest to chest, knee to knee, hand upon throat they fought, for the Turk was game. Now a sabre flashed in the morning light, now a yataghan plunged home with the low, deadly under stroke that the Turkish fighter loves, anon a pistol spoke, or a carbine bit in on the clash of steel. "Allah ill Allah" rang out from infidel throats, only to be answered by the battle cry of the mountain men.

Then came the rout and the vengeful lunge at the backs of the fleeing foes; the appeal for pity and the death stroke for reply and my day with Yankoff ended. My most exciting experience—well, yes, next to a life-long struggle with my creditors I think it was.

A Mango and a Rumor.

A few nights after the fight at San Juan, in Cuba, I decided to make a hurried trip to Daiquiri, where the first landing of American troops had been made, for the purpose of photographing the landing of the siege guns from the steamer Orizaba. Daiquiri was about twenty miles from the front and my old friend James Burton agreed to go with me. As an Englishman, I have often prided myself upon my walking abilities, and a twenty-mile walk did not seem a great undertaking. But under the conditions then prevailing in Cuba, it was a much more difficult feat than I expected. To begin with, owing to lack of transportation facilities, every man had to carry all his belongings, and as my camera was my stock in trade I had to look after that more carefully than after my personal effects. What few roads existed had been cut up by the heavy traffic of the advancing army. Consequently, as may be readily imagined, what with the mud, caused by the heavy rains, and the uncomfortable feeling caused by the alternating tropical showers and intense heat of the sun that dried you off again, this was not the most agreeable walk that I have ever taken.

We finally reached Daiquiri, only to be met with a disappointment. The guns had been transported on different vessels and it seemed that the most vital part was missing, owing to the absence of the particular steamer on which it was ; and as the guns were, therefore, useless, they were not unloaded.

We then concluded to retrace our steps, making a slight detour by way of Siboney. We were warned not to do so on account of the many sharpshooters said to be around ; but as we both believed these reports to be exaggerated, we refused to accept the advice and were about to start back, when a few Spaniards were discovered trying to get around the base of the hill. The Cuban Guard was immediately called out and lined the trenches, whilst we laughed and pooh-poohed, refusing to believe it until the gunboat Wasp, then in the harbor, fired six shells in the vicinity where the Spaniards were supposed to be. We had to admit the possibility of the fact then. However, nothing more happened and after an hour or so we insisted upon leaving and walked first to Siboney. Here, to our horror, we heard the news that "Santiago had surrendered." We were in a nice pickle. Imagine my feelings—Santiago surrendered and Jimmy Hare twelve miles away.

It was then nine o'clock at night. We were so tired that we could hardly move one foot in front of the other and we had had very little to eat since morning. Yet the only thing to do was to start off again and walk through the night, which we accordingly did. Our path took us across the hills to Las Guasimas, where the first scrap had occurred between the Rough Riders and the Spaniards. I am almost tempted to say, where the Rough Riders were ambushed; but President Roosevelt insists that they were not ambushed, and, as he was their Colonel and I only a photographic illustrator, I suppose that he ought to know best. At any rate, it was an ideal spot for an ambuscade. You were hidden from view by the heavy undergrowth for a time; then suddenly you came into an open space and could be seen from neighboring hills for miles around. To my mind, it seemed a very easy thing for an enemy acquainted with the country to head you off and surprise you.

We walked on, occasionally lying down for a short rest, when the hideous land crabs that infest that part would crawl around and over you. Some of these crabs were so large and made such a clatter as they came through the bushes that we thought several times it was a human being coming. This continued nearly to midnight, when suddenly five shots were fired, not at us but, judging from the sound, not very far away. So we decided to drop down where we were and lie in the wet grass until daylight. We had not been lying down very long when a ball as large as a baseball was thrown at us. We realized at once that this was a signal of some kind. Ought we to throw it back, or what?

The sharpshooters that we had ridiculed all day were at last going to get us. Scanning the palm trees in the moonlight, we could almost discern the forms among the branches. My heart—although it seems hard to believe, as I was lying at full length on the ground, still I am prepared to swear to it—my heart came right up from its normal position into my mouth and suddenly fell at my feet. We whispered a little plan of action, should we be attacked before being shot, when another ball was flung. Something had to be done now, so I crawled up to it, although expecting every moment that it would explode. It looked harmless, however, and I finally gathered courage enough to touch it, when I discovered—it was a mango! We were lying under a mango tree and the fruit was being blown down. This did not, however, account for the shots that had been fired, so we decided to lie where we were until morning, when we continued our tramp without having had anything to eat or drink. Eventually, we reached the front once more, only to hear that Santiago had not surrendered. It had been merely a rumor.

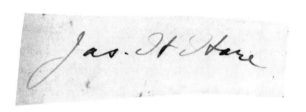

The Break-Up.

It was one of those "good camp nights," when the wolverine's voice, blending sweetly with the vocal efforts of a near-by lynx, softly lulled you to sleep.

Our own dogs had completed their nocturnal prowl and were curled up—as only the Esquimaux malamute can curl—dreaming, no doubt, of the past sled days and the long black lash.

Camped about a quarter of a mile from a wooded slope (that had once been the river bank), opposite a willow patch that made an island in the stream, we were in an awkward position in case of an ice jam.

We were over six hundred miles up the Kuskokwim River—which parallels the Yukon—waiting for the summer's sun to set in motion the silent water. Already the surface was a series of blow-holes, with six or eight inches of flowing water, and we expected every moment to hear the crash that would sound the warning note—the note of freedom for the fettered giant.

It was thus we went to rest on that memorable night, after a hard day of "dull whipsawing," for our boat was nearly completed, and we had put in extra time on the few needed bottom boards.

Dreaming of home faces, chunks of gold and broken lead lines, we were rudely awakened by the expected crash, and it came like no other sound on earth. Popping our heads through the tent flaps, we called to each other, and, even as we did so, the dogs took up the cry and yelped with all their might, as we scrambled out and onto the bank.

Hardly perceptible, so slowly did it move, scarcely credible, so great was its power, as each successive tree on our bank was felled by the tearing edge of the anchor ice, scoring away the bank in its majestic course, craunching, grinding its way, slowly and grandly the river moved ; with now a pause of a moment or two, moments of stifling suspense for us, with forebodings of a jam, breaking in on the intermittent uproar that echoed up and down the river as each lordly spruce was uprooted and carried onward, vassal to the power of the river.

Years can never efface, nor words more vividly portray that moment of nature's working—the night of the "break-up."

Under the alluring light of the half-spent moon we watched the onward flow; slowly it rose, its bosom upheaving with a long-drawn shriek as it burst and threw the fragments up, which piled themselves in fantastic shapes, the whole surface becoming a swirling, sliding mass, while beneath, the river quietly, forcefully moved.

As we turned and looked at each other, we made a feeble attempt at a joke about a chee-chako and a sour-dough; but it was hard to explain our feelings to each other, so we crept again to our spruce-leaf beds, and thought on the wonders we had seen.

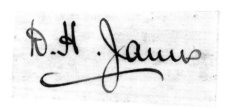

A Trip to New York as a Steward.

Although the following is not an experience of a war correspondent, there was a time when I made the experiment of a trip to New York as a steward in the steerage of a White Star Liner, and I hope the following may be of interest.

It was a miserable wet morning at 5 a.m. when I left my hotel, portmanteau in hand, to join a White Star Liner running between Liverpool and New York, as a steward in the steerage. At 6 a.m. the list of stewards' names was called over, and we were distributed to different parts of the ship. We at once commenced work, and as the great ship was being slowly piloted out of the dock into the river, we made preparations to receive the passengers, who were on tenders in the river waiting for us. At 8 o'clock the tenders came, and we took on about 1600 Swedes, Finns, Spaniards, etc. These were distributed amongst the six sections of the ship. Their first demand was for breakfast, which was at once served. The food was served out to the stewards at the cook's galley right aft, and was carried to the different sections. It was a sight, not uncommon, to see a steward struggling along the slippery deck, carrying a large tin of porridge, or a bucket of tea or coffee (weighing perhaps 50 lbs) suddenly drop everything and make a run for the nearest shelter, sometimes just in time to avoid a great wave and sometimes too late, then having to go to his bunk and change all his clothes.

Perhaps a few lines about our duties would not be out of place. We turned out at 6 o'clock, had coffee, then proceeded to our separate sections, where we laid the tables, and generally prepared for the first meal of the day. About 7 o'clock we got the food from the cook's galley and by 7.30 a.m. were ready. Breakfast being over we went forward for our own breakfast. We then " strapped " up and stood by for inspection by the

Captain, Purser, Doctor and Chief Steward. Dinner came on at 12 o'clock and was finished by 1 o'clock. We had then the afternoon until 5 o'clock, to do as we pleased, after which tea was wanted. After tea was over another " strap up," and inspection was again made. We had then finished. There were also night watches from 12 to 3 and 3 to 6. This was in case of sudden sickness of passengers or fire, etc.

The next morning at Queenstown we took on 200 Irish passengers ; then the fun commenced. It was rather amusing when the Irish boarded. Some were rather " inebriated " and were very evidently celebratι᛫᛫ leaving the old country Cheers for Old Ireland, Irish jigs, with a frequent nip at the whisky bottle, were the rule of the day and night, but when next morning came, as we had then got well into the Atlantic, it brought with it a much different sight. Here and there, dotted along the decks was a sprinkling of the most prominent of the night before, looking so pitiful and mournful, and helping to " swell the ocean." It was a sight to see the avidity with which they took an orange or a lemon, hoping it would cure that awful feeling called sea sickness. Especially amongst the girls was this most noticeable. They seemed as if they were even incapable of moving, and they certainly did not look so smart as when they boarded the ship in their gay dresses the day before; but I wonder what they felt like, when along came some hardened passenger, smoking a cigar or a rank pipe, or when the camera fiend came along, sympathized with them, and then meanly took all the photos possible of them. That passenger must have a collection of photos that money would fail to buy. If seemed to the mere steward so strange a scene—the night before so jolly, everybody looking so happy, the next day, Oh, why did I leave Old Ireland ?

However this could not last forever. It soon came to an end, and the stewards were kept busy feeding them. Then the concertina was again called into use, and dancing by all was the order of the day.

Then the Irish passengers began to intermix with passengers from the cold barren north, and many an Irishman wished to show, and did show, the big, strong, unwieldy Swede how to fight in " Ireland's way," and many a contest was won and lost. Then the ladies' man came along and experienced the warmth of the Irish girl, but he was never sure when the Irish boy would come along. When he did come it was with wrath and hot jealousy, and then it was " look out " for the poor ladies' man. After a few experiences the Swedes began to be very diplomatic, and soon they were all to be seen together.

At last one night we felt the ship stop, and heard the anchor chain rattling. We then knew we were outside New York harbour, and when we all went on deck and saw the lights of the entrance to the harbour, we felt sorry that the morrow would end a most delightful and interesting trip.

Next morning everything was hurry and bustle. The inspecting doctor came aboard, inspected all the passengers and crew, all those who had not been vaccinated were at once operated upon, all the holds disinfected, and the ship declared free from infectious diseases, etc.

We then steamed leisurely to the entrance to the Custom House. The girls who had looked so pitiful such a short time before were all gaily dressed, and everyone seemed pleased. All the misery they had experienced was forgotten, and their only thought was they had reached New York at last. Then nobody seemed to know where their luggage was, and the poor, hard-worked steward had to set things right. Then the gangways were ready and with a final cheer and parting the passengers went—to meet again no one knows where and when. Thus ended a most interesting experience.

FREDERIC WHITING.

A Veldt Vendetta.

" Give us your most exciting war experience," said the Editor of this unique publication. Here's mine. I nearly died with the Irish Brigade in Natal. It was my own fault. I discovered a most bitter feeling among the Durban Light Infantry towards the Dublin Fusiliers. I investigated the affair, and knew enough of the facts to take part in the climax. It was almost fatal. It all arose from a truck load of beer. Among the many irregular corps raised in Natal was the Durban Light Infantry. One of the Officers was a Pietermaritzburg brewer. Two months of hard fighting, in fearful heat, convinced this malster that Maritzburg ale was preferable to Frere Creek water. He consulted his directorate, and the answer was two truck loads of beer, consigned to the men of the Durban Light Infantry with the compliments of the brewery. The Durban Light Infantry antici-pated the arrival of the consignment and foolishly boasted of their coming feast. Two dozen hogsheads of the best Natal brew were sufficient for a brigade. They expressed their intention of treating their pals in the other corps, mostly irregulars. Camped close to the siding were the Dublin Fusiliers, common looters and much below the status of the irregulars in the eyes of the D. L. I. Squads of Dubs daily and nightly guarded the supply trains in the switches. Beer was as scarce as snow. Every hour of every day for over a week a Durban Light Infantry man examined the incoming trucks. " It's beer they are looking for," said a Dublin sergeant, and next day every man in the regiment was thinking of the affair. The facts leaked out. The Dubs also awaited the beer with interest. It came one evening, when the Durban Light Infantry were on a reconnaisance. Before dark there was not an empty sardine tin or salmon can in the camp or on the creek, but they were not sufficient to hold the contents of one truck. The cavalry lines lent a score of horse buckets in exchange for six pails of the frothy liquid. There was wild hilarity in the Irish camp until long past midnight. A full half of one company was locked up by the guard. The canvas gaol would hold no more, so scores of names were taken and when the sergeants failed to get the names they took the numbers from the shoulder straps. Ten Dubs. on the defaulters' list would any morning bring from Colonel Cooper's lips a severe reprimand to the whole battalion for its lack of discipline. On the morning after the beer he was faced by 200 repentent and sorry looking defaulters. He gave the lot pack drill for a week and stopped their stipends for a whole month. When a squad of the Durban Light Infantry called at the siding for the casks they merrily wheeled away six filled with water from the creek. A sergeant saw the following chalked on the truck and he left the balance of the consignment. The couplet ran :—

"To the Dear Little Innocents."

" We looting Dubs ; we stole your tubs of beer."

" You were the mugs—so pardon us our leer."

This was the beginning of the vendetta.

The brewery heard of the theft, and they replaced the consignment. By this time the army had advanced to Colenso and again the Dubs guarded the railway sidings. When the second batch arrived the Durban Light Infantrymen were on watch. The trucks could not be unloaded that day so a sergeant and twelve men were sent to guard them all night—with fixed bayonets. At night three officers arrived. One, plainly a major from the crown on his shoulder strap, asked the Durban Light Infantry sergeant what he was doing there with such a guard. He explained.

" Fall your men in and follow me," said the Major. He took them down the bank of the dark Tugela, and pointing to the other side, he whispered, " Guard this ford with your life. Don't challenge, shoot carefully every man or beast which dares to cross. You will be relieved at midnight." The sergeant and his squad zealously guarded the stream. At midnight the officer of the round arrived. " What are you men doing here ?" he said. The sergeant explained. " Get back to your trucks," replied the officer, " and if you hurry you may save some of that beer." They were too late.

The Durban Light Infantry were saved the indignity of wheeling away dirty water, but for the second time the Dubs were utilising empty tins from the rubbish heaps and even horse buckets. Among the 100 defaulters paraded next morning was a Major's servant. The charges against him were: " Drunk and disorderly, and further with having stolen his master's tunic and appropriated the same to his own use."

The vendetta ended with the departure of the Durban Light Infantry, but it proved nearly fatal to several others besides myself who knew the facts.

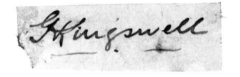

Treasure Trove.

A subsidiary problem in the great game, intimately associated therewith from time immemorial to infinitude, is the thirst question.

The man whose trade is war, either as a soldier or otherwise, has had —and always will have—many encounters with this comprehensive enemy. This, doubtless, in many people's minds, accounts for his susceptibility to the charms of Bacchus when the multi-coloured libations to that hilarious god are procurable.

These remarks do not apply to amateur or induced thirst, but to the hot-drawn genuine article ; the drought which during and towards the end of the day commences at one's lips, extends throughout the whole alimentary canal, permeates the capillaries of one's extremities, giving one the sensation or impression of being a huge bath sponge wrung out, hung up, and forgotten for all the summer, a tout ensemble provocative of cerulean, if husky, profanity.

Such was my state and condition on a certain night in November, 1899. The fight of Modder River was not twenty hours old, yet the yellow-brown dusty plain, with its line of green thorn and mimosa bush marking the river bed, stank with a stench almost tangible. Incidentally I had fired over a hundred rounds, also the earth had suddenly risen up and kicked me as the old horse fell dead with a bullet through his off-fore and heart, and I was one big ache. I had not reached the river, and a "drink" of pea soup " water " had been my only portion throughout the livelong day. I was possessed of a thirst the memory of which should live forever and be perpetuated by a colossal monument in the capital city of the realm of fantasy ; my lips grow dry at the remembrance of it.

Sunrise came at last, the river was half a mile away and I rode down towards it with the determination to drink or " bust." That portion of the scattered hamlet lying on the south bank had formed the centre of the enemy's position on the previous day and had been subjected to the concentrated fire of our field batteries. An hotel, the erstwhile resort of Kimberley " week-enders," was a blackened, shattered ruin ; it had lit the whole scene at the tail end of the action the night before, and was now an agglomeration of twisted, torn corrugated iron, shattered walls, shot-ripped trees, and litter indescribable.

A blue-eyed boy in command of a patrol of the 9th Lancers stood disconsolately surveying the wreck as I rode up. I knew that he and his men were in the same case as myself. We entered what had been the bar and billiard room : A shattered billiard table, broken bottles and glassware, burnt timber, seats, bricks, and dust. " Nothing here!" he remarked. Meanwhile, I sounded the floor with my heel till at last I found—what I thought I should find. In most South African hotels the stock of liquor is kept in a cellar located somewhere near the bar and easily get-at-able. Ripping the remains of linoleum aside I lifted the trap-door and ran down the steps. Bottles—bottles with a red pyramid on the label, gold, yellow, red-topped ; bottles of all sorts and shapes !

I climbed those steps again, with difficulty. The scoffer will say " that's easily understood," but for once he is wrong. It was outside, right down to my putties and around my shoulder blades. Armour plated with Bass and Clicquot till I could hardly breathe or walk, mounting was difficult, and I didn't trouble the river ; but riding back to camp, clambering off with my load, the glint in the eyes of the boys when the whisper " beer " ran—marconigram-like—through the dust-dry mess is a memory which will live in the mind of

How I Was Nearly Beheaded.

Perhaps the most interesting ten minutes of my life was the occasion when I was being tried by a very irregular drum-head court-martial and had every reason to believe that the separation of my head from my body was about to be effected without superfluous formality or delay.

It was in Northern Albania in the winter of 1878. The Treaty of Berlin had been signed, and by its terms the town and district of Gusinje had been ceded to Montenegro. Gusinje—a dangerous centre of Mohammedan fanaticism—was at that time the headquarters of the Albanian League, a Mohammedan organisation, whose aim it was to defy the arrangement that had been entered into by the Great Powers, to obtain autonomy for Albania and to resist by force the cession of Gusinje to Montenegro. So Gusinje, though Montenegrin territory by treaty, was occupied by ten thousand resolute Mussulmans, while Montenegro had an equal force encamped a few miles off, just within her frontier.

Another journalist and myself were anxious to visit Gusinje at this juncture, so as to get in touch with the League. We had ridden across the snow-covered mountains from Scutari through the country of the Roman Catholic Clementi tribe. Nik Leka, the Clementi chieftain, was our friend, so we were safe with these wild highlanders, who at that time were undecided as to whether they should join the League or no, and so observed a strict neutrality—that is, they used quite impartially to cut the throats of Leaguesmen or Montenegrins who came their way, so as to possess themselves of the richly-ornamented, gold-inlaid weapons which many of these people carry.

After travelling for three days we came to a lonely hut on a high ridge at the extreme limit of the Clementi country, whence we looked down upon the town of Gusinje some thousands of feet below us and about tow hours, journey distant. An Italian Franciscan from the neighbouring mission station, Kastrate, accompanied us as far as the hut, and here we awaited the reply to a letter that we had sent to Ali Bey, the leader of the Leaguesmen in Gusinje. The reply was brought to us at about midday and was thus worded : " If you two people will guarantee that the Montenegrin force retires within two days you may come here. If you cannot do this you had better not come." This was not reassuring and the Franciscan, knowing the ways of the land, proved to us that to proceed to Gusinje was to court certain death. We therefore decided to return to the Franciscan Mission, but before doing so we ate our midday meal in the hut.

In conformance with the invariable custom of the country we had handed over our weapons to our Albanian host, and our rifles and pistols were hanging with his own upon the wall. We were sitting Turkish fashion on the floor, enjoying our roasted goat, our backs being turned to the open door, when I saw the faces of my host and of his wife change as if a sudden danger had come, and on turning my head I saw, filling up the doorway, about a dozen Bosnian and Albanian Mussulmans armed to the teeth. As we rose to our feet, several of them entered the hut quickly and stood between us and our weapons. " Ali Bey is willing that these men should come to Gusinje," said their spokesman. " We have been sent to escort them in."

Then ensued a curious conversation, the Franciscan translating the Albanian tongue for us into dog-Latin, our usual medium of intercourse. " This is a trap," said he at last. " They do not come from Ali Bey. They have brought no letter from him. To go with them means death. But do not at once refuse to accompany them; argue the question. You are lost unless we gain time."

So we carried on a parley until at last the men waxed impatient; for they abandoned the attempt to persuade us, and addressing our host, told him plainly that they had been sent to cut our heads off, as it had been discovered that we were Russian spies. Had our Clementi friends credited this statement our position would have been hopeless, for they hated Russians with a bitter hatred.

In my best dog-Latin I explained what we were. It was an argument on which our lives hung. Soon our host, believing in us, bravely took our part and declared that we were no Russians. Then the men from Gusinje talked with one another for a little while and arrived at a decision. They would kill us there and then. Well do I remember the exact words used by the Franciscan as he interpreted their words: "*O amici,*" he said, "*multum est periculum pro vobis. Ille homo dixit ad alium Nune est tempus intercidere illos homines.*" The men had their yataghans ready drawn, and some had their pistols at full cock. I think it passed through the minds of both of us Englishmen, as we caught each other's eyes, that all that was left for us to do was to make a combined rush, attempt the disarmament of one or two of the men and at least make a fight for it.

But the delay that had been gained by the protracted parley saved us. One of the Gusinje men without raised a warning cry, and looking through the door we perceived a Clementi highlander, rifle in hand, standing on a rocky height hard by. He made a sign with his hand and a look of relief came to our host's face. " Cease this foolish talk of killing these men," he said. " These Englishmen are the friends of the Clementi and we will protect them with our lives." A number of armed Clementi now appeared on the sky-line, and the men of Gusinje, realising that they were outnumbered, sullenly marched off through the deep snow. A " regrettable incident " occurred lower down the pass an hour or so later. I was told afterwards that there had been a fray, in which two of our would-be executioners lost their lives, the Clementi coveting the valuable weapons which the men carried.

.O

Bleary and weary and drear,
Half way between Heaven and Hell,
Is the desolate region of NOWHERE,
Where the unhappy NOBODIES dwell.

Nonentities only were they,
Doing naught good or ill in the World,
And so for their negative fault,
To the NEGATIVE Limbo were hurled.

O how can these poor souls inhabit
A region so utterly slow,
Where life is an endless NEGATION,
Existence an infinite NO !

They sow the whirlwinds with NOTHINGS,
Reap harvests of impotent NOTS,
Their sphere is one vast NEGATORIUM,
Where NEGATE they in separate lots.

" We—the emptiest of Zeros in Space,
Ye Gods," they cry in distress,
" Give thy suppliants *some* AFFIRMATION,
If it only be *one* little YES !

" We have NONSENSES only for senses ;
For language we have but a NAY.

O grant us our portion of YESNESS,
If it be but the ghost of a YEA !

" In *some* World two NEGATIVES make
An AFFIRMATIVE—scientists *say* (?)
But two of our NO's could not make one,
Did they work for a year and a day.

" Yet thou knowest that our NO's are the **NOEST,**
Our NOTS are the NOTTEST of NOTS ;
We are NOBODIES only, forgive us
For talking this rottest of rots ! "

Saving a Column.

At the time during the South African war when there were grave fears that a serious rising would take place in Cape Colony, I was attached to one of the flying columns operating under General French. Everything was sacrificed to obtain the utmost possible limit of mobility. Wheeled transport was left behind, all supplies being carried on pack mules. We marched from before dawn until after dusk and the route was strewn with the carcases of horses that had succumbed from sheer exhaustion. Hundreds of men who were thus deprived of mounts tramped wearily along in the wake of the lightning-like column. Rapid marching, however, did not mean severe fighting ; and for nearly two months the enemy evaded engagement until it seemed as though we were chasing a phantom foe.

When in the mountainous district of Graft Remet, the scouts at last located a Boer commando. The harass of the march had by this time played havoc with the column, men were worn out and haggard, and horses were almost incapable of any pace above a trot. We were indeed a torn and tattered remnant, but the realisation that after all there was an enemy to engage came at even this, the eleventh and a half hour, as a refreshing stimulant.

It was midday when the incident of the march occurred. The chief of the scouts, a Dutch sergeant, came, galloping back to the advance guard with the information that Kritzinger's commando was only ten miles ahead. Men who were almost dropping out of their saddles stiffened up at the prospect of a " scrap," drooping horses were gently spurred into activity, and the column set off at a smart pace which was something less than a gallop but something more than a trot.

Not far away was a lofty mountain littered with boulders each one of which gave the advancing army the impression that it concealed the lurking enemy. The commanding officer promptly sent forward a patrol of twenty men with orders to thoroughly scout the surrounding country. I accompanied the little force which was officered by a young lieutenant who had won considerable distinction in the early part of the war. In skirmishing order we cautiously rode over a little plain flanked on one side by a long, low-lying ridge and upon the other side bounded by the mountain slopes. "It is hardly worth while bothering about the ridge," said the officer, adding, "We had better make for the mountain. That is the place where the Boers will shelter and it will take us a long time to thoroughly search the land. The column is not far behind and no time can be wasted." So we abandoned the ridge on the far side of the column. As we approached the mountain no signs of the enemy were visible. Soon we were toiling up the steep slopes warily threading our way in and out of the great stone boulders.

After an hour's steady climbing, leading our horses all the while, we reached the summit of the mountain, but still there were no traces of the enemy that we knew were not far away. The lieutenant took out his field glasses and intently scanned the country. Suddenly he excitedly exclaimed: "I see them—look! they are over there!" As he spoke he pointed to the low-lying ridge away on the far side of the road along which column was marching. Here lay waiting in ambush a commando of nearly a thousand Boers with rifles ready sighted to pour a stream of lead into the rapidly oncoming column. Now only a mile separated the two forces; the distance would shortly be lessened to within deadly range. The boyish features of the lieutenant pallored with the pain of anxiety, for he realised that the men of the patrol having failed in their work must now look down upon a terrible scene of carnage. For a few moments he seemed absolutely incapable of action, the prospect of impending disaster having completely overwhelmed him.

Then recovering himself he quietly gave orders to the patrol to open fire on the advancing column as a warning of danger ahead. It was the stern action of a genuine hero, but the consequences were disastrous to the little patrol on the mountain top. As soon as the rifles cracked the first volley we saw the column extend into one long line, the right flank of which speedily secured a commanding position on the range of mountains. A heavy fire encircled the little space of ground which we occupied, and within a quarter of an hour the shells pelted the boulders around. One by one the men of the patrol fell ; soon only a lieutenant, a single trooper and myself remained on the mountain top. But we anxiously waited and watched until the Boers evacuated the ridge and fled in all directions. Then, with the knowledge that a disaster had not only been averted but a victory won, we went down the mountain side, leaving behind the few men who had been sacrificed in order that the greater number might be saved. While, however, the stern old commanding officer complimented the brave young lieutenant upon the incisive action which extricated the column from a disaster that would have meant annihilation, he could not repress a kindly reminder that the duty of a scout was to scout ridges as well as mountain tops.

Lancelot X. Lawton

"Waiting," Tokio, March 21st., 04.

Waiting in Tokio's all very well
But we have had waiting galore,
No one's been here less than twenty days
And many have been three score;
Waiting for "permits" which never arrive
Waiting to get away
Waiting and loafing and drinking and smoking
Honestly (?) earning our pay!

Some from England, some from the States,
Others from "Furrin parts,"
Have collected here from the ends of the earth
With the same intent in their hearts.
There's a sameness about our doings,
There's a sameness about our meals,
There's a sameness about the depression,
The depression that every one feels.

Jinrikisha drive after breakfast,
To tiffin by 'rickisha, too,
"Any news at the Legation ?"
"Only a letter or two."
Call at the Foreign Office,
Cards on your hostess last night,
Look up a "Jap friend in the know"
To hear more about the last fight.

You've little knowledge of " noospaper men,"
And of war correspondents, too ;
Don't harden your hearts as Pharoah did,
But let the whole lot see it through.
Why should you want to stop us ?
We are no Russian spies ;
We've come in a friendly spirit,
From nations with kindred ties.

And it's possible, too, that before the end
We'll be fighting side by side,
Put that in your pipe and smoke it,
Whatever else you may decide.
This *may* be a war of nations
And *you* can't afford to lose ;
A friend in need is a friend indeed.
(If I'm speaking too plain, you'll excuse.)

But when all's said and done we won't grumble,
You've done us exceedingly well ;
A month or two hence there'll be fever
And "fun " and fighting and Hell !
So here's to our Tokio hosts and friends,
And we thank you once more and again,
And many a man will remember this time
When he's trying to sleep in the rain.

"R. T. P.'s."

Julius Caesar was seated on a rock writing his message to the Roman Senate.

"Veni, vidi, vici," he wrote, and then paused.

"Great Caesar!" said the telegraph operator, "the censor won't let you send that message through."

"Why not?" asked the great general.

"Because," replied the telegraph operator, "in the first place you say, 'I came,' thus betraying military movements. In the second place you say, 'I saw,' betraying a military observation; and in the third place you say, 'I conquered,' thereby betraying military secrets and putting the defeated enemy in possession of an important fact. And besides, the censor will think that 'Veni' is a code word."

"Then I am not permitted to send a code message?" asked Imperial Caesar haughtily.

"Not on your life," said the telegraph operator.

"Then," said Caesar, "I will write a code of my own."

Whereupon, Julius sat down and wrote the Roman Civil Code.

"Are you a Christian?" asked the war correspondent of the Japanese whom he was examining with a view of engaging him to be his interpreter.

"No," said the Japanese. "Are you?"

AFTER MANY YEARS.

A War Time Play in One Act.

Time. 1950.

Scene. Veranda of Imperial Hotel, Tokyo.

Characters.

Captain Pat Mac Hugh.   Sometime war correspondent for British newspaper long ago bought in by Johnny Morgan. Character heavy, with long white whiskers and bald head.

Frederick Palmer.   Juvenile lead.   Also with long white whiskers and bald head.   War correspondent, but not working on the job.

Bobby Collins.   Expatriate American working Reuter's Syndicate for all it is worth.   Long white whiskers touching ground, bent with age, gout in both feet and with cracked voice.

Curtain rises and discovers these three seated on piazza drinking Scotch and soda.

Mac Hugh.   (Stroking beard and in trembling voice.)   "Ah, 'tis now forty-six years, forty-six years, since I came out to report the Japanese-Russian war.   Forty-six years and it seems but yesterday."

Palmer.   (Voice cracked with age and leaning heavily on cane.) "Have you bought your outfit yet, Mack ? "

Mac Hugh.   "Well, almost everything.   I don't think the outfit I am buying now is as good as the one I got when I first landed.   But that has long ago rotted away and naught now is left but my patent folding bed.   Ah me, how time flies."

Palmer.   "Have you heard the news ?   They tell me at the War Office that we are going to get pass number 3456 to-morrow."

Mac Hugh.   (with irritation.)   " I am tired of going over there all the time to get passes.   Why don't they issue one pass and make it good for twenty years ? "

Palmer.   " Sh, not so loud.   Remember the secret police.   I had a hunch from the American Minister to-day—by the way, he is the grandson of Griscom, who was Minister when we first arrived—that we would start for Manchuria some time next July."

Collins.   " Manchuria, where is Manchuria ? "

Palmer.   " 'Tis where the war is going on."

Collins.   " And what is war ? "

Mac Hugh. (low voice.) "Poor old man ! Forty-six years of riding back and forth in a rickisha between the hotel and the War Office have done this. He has forgotten everything. He thinks he is a rickisha."

Stranger just landed from ship at Yokohama suddenly walks out on veranda.

Stranger. " Pardon me, gentlemen, but happening to overhear your conversation I thought I had best tell you that the Russian-Japanese war was ended thirty-nine years ago."

Mac Hugh. (faltering voice.) " Ended thirty-nine years ago ! And the War Office never told us ! "

Collins. " Rick-sha, plees mister, rick-sha."

Palmer and Mac Hugh fall into each other's arms and weep. Collins hies himself for a ride over to the War Office. Music of Imperial Guard Band playing for the Saturday night dinner heard in distance. Red fire.

Curtain.

> Bright-eyed and brave, he went off to the war,
> But now by the Yalu he's lying;
> Dead? you ask. No, but a war correspondent,
> Which accounts, you see, for the lying.

THE NEW MANAGER (E. FLAIG)

Will sell at public auction,

Field Kits

&

Estates,

Left in his hands by the

WAR CORRESPONDENTS,

Including all the articles named below and many others. All field equipment articles in prime condition, having never been used. Articles include, patent folding bath tubs (Maxwell patent); patent folding camp cots; patent folding camp chairs; patent reversible double back action sleeping bag lined with wool and moths; patent collapsible tents; Brill's patent rain proof dog shelter; patent soup kettle and collar box; patent skittle and wash bowl combined, very unique, Gordon Smith patentee; revolvers; belts; medicines; chamois shirts; flannel shirts; wool shirts; corduroy suits; Egan's overcoat; five Melton Prior pies slightly damaged; saddles; blankets; mirrors; pictures and mottoes for tents; glass ware; Maxwell's patent mahogany bureau and dresser for field service with attachment in back which properly approached becomes a piano in the daytime and a bed at night; tent carpets; four dozen seltzer syphons; one small note book; three lead pencils; two hundred quarts rye whisky; four hundred quarts Scotch whisky; spades; axes; mosquito bar netting; Mac Hugh's quick fire rifle cannon arranged to be carried in belt but could be mounted in rickisha; bedding; towels; tooth brushes; boxes; trunks; field rolls; hot rolls; tinned meats of all description; one bottle ink; two thousand bottles bourbon whisky; Davis patent field furnace for use in tent; Palmer's patent campaigning sectional house, with fence and garden; Knight's patent camp oak tree that can be carried in a field roll, set up in front of tent giving a comfortable shade and taken down all in two hours; the Jimmy Hare patent well boring apparatus insuring fine supply of drinking water for washing clothes on the march; and many other articles of a similar kind.

THE OPPORTUNITY OF A LIFE TIME.

EVERYTHING WILL BE SOLD.

COME EARLY AND INSPECT GOODS.

DO NOT FORGET TIME AND PLACE.

A Camera and a Journey.

I journeyed all day from Yokohama to Kobe to catch a steamer for Chemulpo, which last city is on the road to Seoul. I journeyed all day and all night from Kobe to Nagasaki to catch a steamer for Chemulpo. I journeyed back all day from Nagasaki to Moji to catch a steamer for Chemulpo. On Monday morning, in Moji, I bought my ticket for Chemulpo, to sail on Monday afternoon. To-day is Wednesday, and I am still trying to catch a steamer for Chemulpo. And thereby hangs a tale of war and disaster, which runs the gamut of the emotions from surprise and anger to sorrow and brotherly love, and which culminates in arrest, felonious guilt and confiscation of property, to say nothing of monetary fines or alternative imprisonment.

For know that Moji is a fortified place, and one is not permitted to photograph " land or water scenery." I did not know it, and I photographed neither land nor water scenery, but I know it now, just the same.

Having bought my ticket at the Osaka Shosen Kaisha office, I tucked it into my pocket and stepped out of the door. Came four coolies carrying a bale of cotton. Snap went my camera. Five little boys at play—snap again. A line of coolies carrying coal—and again snap, and last snap. For a middle-aged Japanese man, in European clothes and great perturbation, fluttered his hands prohibitively before my camera. Having performed this function, he promptly disappeared.

" Ah, it is not allowed," I thought, and, calling my ricksha-man, I strolled along the street.

Later, passing by a two-story frame building, I noticed my middle-aged Japanese standing in the doorway. He smiled and beckoned me to enter. " Some chin chin and tea," thought I, and obeyed. But alas ! It was destined to be too much chin-chin and no tea at all. I was in the police station. The middle-aged Japanese was what the American hobo calls a " fly cop."

Great excitement ensued. Captains, lieutenants and ordinary police-men all talked at once and ran hither and thither. I had run into a hive of blue uniforms, brass buttons, and cutlasses. The populace clustered like flies at doors and windows to gape at the Russian spy. At first it was all very ludicrous. " Capital to while away some of the time ere my steamer departs," was my judgment ; but when I was taken to an upper room and the hours began to slip by, I decided that it was serious.

I explained that I was going to Chemulpo. " In a moment," said the interpeter. I showed my ticket, my passport, my card, my credentials ; and always and invariably came the answer, " In a moment." Also, the inter-preter stated that he was very sorry. He made special trips upstairs to tell me he was very sorry. Every time I told him I was going to Chemulpo, he expressed his sorrow, until we came to vie with each other, I in explain-ing my destination, he in explaining the state and degree of his emotion regarding me and my destination.

And so it went. The hour of tiffin had long gone by. I had had an early breakfast. But my appetite waited on his " In a moment," till after-noon was well along. Then came the police examination, replete with searching questions concerning myself, my antecedents, and every member of my family, all of which information was gravely written down. An unappeasable interest in my family was displayed. The remotest relatives were hailed with keen satisfaction and placed upon paper. The exact ascer-tainment of their antecedents and birthplaces seemed necessary to the point at issue, namely, the snaps I had taken of the four coolies carrying cotton, the five little boys playing, and the string of coal-coolies.

Next came my movements since my arrival in Japan. " Why did you go to Kobe ? " " To go to Chemulpo," was my answer ; and in this fash-ion I explained my presence in the various cities of Japan. I made mani-fest that my only reason for existence was to go to Chemulpo ; but their conclusion from my week's wandering was that I had no fixed place of abode. I began to shy.   The last time the state of my existence had been so designated it had been followed by a thirty-day's imprisonment in a vagrant's cell.   Chemulpo suddenly grew dim and distant, and began to fade beyond the horizon of my mind.

"What is your rank?" was the initial question of the next stage of the examinaiton.

I was nobody, I explained, a mere citizen of the United States ; though I felt like saying that my rank was that of traveler for Chemulpo.   I was given to understand that by rank was meant business profession.

"Traveling to Chemulpo," I said was my business; and when they looked puzzled I meekly added that I was only a correspondent.

Next, the hour and the minute that I made the three exposures.   Were they of land and water scenery ?   No, they were of people.   What people ?   Then I told of the four coolies carrying cotton, the five small boys playing, and the string of coal-coolies.   Did I stand with my back to the water while making the pictures ?   Did I stand with my back to the land ?   Somebody had informed them that I had taken pictures in Nagasaki (a police lie, and they sprang many such on me). I strenuously denied it.   Besides, it had rained all the time I was in Nagasaki.   What other pictures had I taken in Japan ?   Three ; two of Mount Fuji, one of a man selling tea at a railway station.   Where were the pictures ? In the camera.   Along with the four coolies carrying cotton, the five small boys playing, and the string of coal-coolies ?   Yes.

Now about those four coolies carrying cotton, the five small boys playing, and the string of coal-coolies ?   And then they threshed through the details of the three exposures, up and down, back and forth and cross-ways, till I wished that the coal-coolies, cotton-coolies and small boys had never been born.   I have dreamed about them ever since, and I know I shall dream about them until I die.

Why did I take the pictures ?   Because I wanted to.   Why did I want to ?   For my pleasure.   Why for my pleasure ?

Pause a moment, gentle reader, and consider.   What answer could you give to such a question concerning any act you have ever performed? Why do you do anything? Because you want to, because it is your pleasure. An answer to the question "Why do you perform an act for your pleasure?" would constitute an epitome of psychology. Such an answer would go down to the roots of being, for it involves impulse, volition, pain, pleasure, sensation, gray matter, nerve fibers, free will and determinism, and all the vast fields of speculation wherein man has floundered since the day he dropped down out of the trees and began to seek out the meaning of things.

And I, a insignificant traveler on my way to Chemulpo, was asked this question in the Moji police station through the medium of a seventh-rate interpreter. Nay, an answer was insisted upon. Why did I take the pictures because I wanted to, for my pleasure? I wished to take them. Why? Because the act of taking them would make me happy. Why would the act of taking them make me happy? Because it would give me pleasure. But why would it give me pleasure? I hold no grudge against the policeman who examined me at Moji, yet I hope that in the life to come he will encounter the shade of Herbert Spencer and be informed just why, precisely, I took the pictures of the four coolies carrying cotton, the five small boys playing, and the string of coal-coolies.

Now concerning my family, were my sisters older than I or younger? The change in the line of questioning was refreshing even though it was perplexing. But ascertained truth is safer than metaphysics, and I answered blithely. Had I a pension from the government? a salary? Had I a medal of service? of merit? Was it an American camera? Was it instantaneous? Was it mine?

To cut a simple narrative short, I pass on from this sample of the examination I underwent, to the next step in the proceedings, which was the development of the film.

Guarded by a policeman and accompanied by the interpreter, I was taken through the streets of Moji to a native photographer. I described the location of the three pictures on the film of ten. Observe the simplicity of it. These three pictures he cut out and developed, the seven other exposures, or possible exposures, being returned to me undeveloped. They might have contained the secret of the fortifications of Moji, for all the policemen knew ; and yet I was permitted to carry them away with me, and I have them now. For the peace of Japan, let me declare that they contain only pictures of Fuji and tea-sellers.

I asked permission to go to my hotel and pack my trunks—in order to be ready to catch the steamer for Chemulpo. Permission was accorded, and my luggage accompanied me back to the police station, where I was again confined in the upper room, listening to the " In a moment " of the interpreter and harping my one note that I wanted to go to Chemulpo.

In one of the intervals the interpreter remarked," I know great American correspondent formerly.

" What was his name ? " I asked politely.

" Benjamin Franklin," came the answer ; and I swear, possibly because I was thinking of Chemulpo, that my face remained as graven as an image.

The arresting officer now demanded that I should pay for developing the incriminating film, and my declining to do so caused him not a little consternation.

" I am very sorry," said the interpreter, and there were tears in his voice ; " I inform you cannot go to Chemulpo. You must go to Kokura." Which last place I learned was a city a few miles in the interior.

" Baggage go ?" I asked.

" You pay ? " he countered. I shook my head.

" Baggage go not," he announced.

" And I go not," was my reply.

I was led downstairs into the main office. My luggage followed. The police surveyed it. Everybody began to talk at once. Soon they were shouting. The din was terrific, the gestures terrifying. In the midst of it, I asked the interpreter what they had decided to do and he answered, shouting to make himself heard, that they were talking it over.

Finally, rickshaws were impressed, and bag and baggage transferred to the depot. Alighting at the depot at Kokura, more delay was caused by my declining to leave my luggage in the freight office. In the end it was carted along with me to the police station, where it became a spectacle for all the officials.

Here I underwent an examination before the Public Procurator of the Kokura District Court. The interpreter began very unhappily, as follows :

" Customs different in Japan from America, therefore you must not tell any lies."

Then was threshed over once again all the details of the four coolies carrying cotton, the five small boys playing, and the string of coal-coolies ; and I was commited, to appear for trial next morning.

And next morning, bareheaded, standing, I was tried by three solemn, black capped judges. The affair was very serious ; I had committed a grave offense, and the Public Procurator stated that while I did not merit a prison sentence I was, nevertheless, worthy of a fine.

After an hour's retirement the judges achieved a verdict. I was to pay a fine of five yen, and Japan was to get the camera. All of which was eminently distasteful to me, but I managed to extract a grain of satisfaction from the fact that they quite forgot to mulct me of the five yen. There is trouble brewing for somebody because of those five yen. There is the judgment. I am a free man. But how are they to balance accounts?

In the evening, at the hotel, the manager of the hotel, a Japanese, handed me a card, upon which was transcribed. " Reporter of the Osaka Asahi Shimbun."

I met him in the reading-room, a slender, spectacled, silk-gowned man, who knew not one word of English. The manager acted as interpreter. The reporter was very sorry for my predicament. He expressed the regret of twenty other native correspondents in the vicinity, who, in turn, represented the most powerful newspapers in the Empire. He had come to offer their best offices, also to interview me.

The law was the law, he said, and the decree of the court could not be set aside ; but there were ways of getting around the law. The voice of the newspapers was heard in the land. He and his fellow correspondents would petition the Kokura judges to auction off the camera, he and his associates to attend and bid it in at a nominal figure. Then it would give them the greatest pleasure to present my camera (or the Mikado's, or theirs) to me with their compliments.

I could have thrown my arms about him then and there—not for the camera, but for brotherhood, as he himself expressed it the next moment, because we were brothers in the craft. Then we had tea together and talked over the prospects of war. The nation of Japan he likened to a prancing and impatient horse, the government to the rider, endeavoring to restrain the fiery steed. The people wanted war, the newspapers wanted war, public opinion clamored for war ; and war the government would eventually have to give them.

We parted as brothers part, and, without wishing him any ill luck, I should like to help him out of a hole some day in the United States. And here I remain in my hotel, wondering if I'll ever see my camera again, and trying to find another steamer for Chemulpo.

P. S.—Just received a dispatch from the United States Minister at Tokio. As an act of courtesy the Minister of Justice will issue orders to-day to restore my camera.

P. S.—And a steamer sails to-morrow for Chemulpo.

Nippon Banzaï.

" Dai Nippon Teikoku Banzai," how the cry recalls the memory of the most picturesque fight I have seen—the attack on the East gate of Pekin by the Japanese in 1900.   Soon after daybreak they had endeavoured to blow up the gate but the Chinese fire from the gatehouse and wall was too hot.   Then they shelled it with 64 guns but little or no impression was made upon the solid centuries old masonry.

General Fukushima had determined to make another attempt to blow up the gate as soon as the darkness would give cover to his sappers. The firing had ceased, and we could see the operations in progress for the final effort that was shortly to be made.   The houses on both sides of the long street had by this time been occupied by the Japanese soldiers, and as darkness came on many of the men lay down to get a little sleep, and I had just dropped off when I was awakened by a loud explosion, quickly followed by another. I knew what that meant.   It was the gate being blown up at last.

In a few seconds, outside the doors, the Japanese were passing up at the double.   Everything was awake now.   There they were running forward with their " One, two, One, two " war chant.   The Chinese had opened fire again from the wall, almost as hot as that wherewith they had greeted us in the morning.   The Japanese had to get along by creeping close to the houses on each side.   It was a fine night, and the moon had just risen. There was no use in returning the Chinese fire.   On they went on both sides of the street, taking advantage of every projecting corner.   Gusts of bullets stormily swept down the street.   Then the men halted at the last corner.   There was a broad open space until the gatehouse itself was reached   The fire was very severe on the bridge.   The Japanese were pressed close to the wall behind every coign of protection.   But my goodness, how they did enjoy it! How they sang and cheered. It was sufficient to shout " Nippon Banzai " and a ringing cheer answered.

They went forward across the open space in batches. I went with the rush of a lot of them, and did a hundred yards in my record time. From the high wall above us the Chinese kept firing away. There was deep shadow below outside the walls, and when we got under the heavy gate there was protection from fire. And thus a corner of the courtyard was passed. Here the scene was stirring and dramatic to a degree. The Chinese still kept firing from the high walls above us, every shot making a hundred echoes in the courtyard; the white uniforms of the Japanese showed up even in the inky shadows, and their fixed bayonets gleamed. There was a rattle of accoutrements and of steel upon stone, and all the time they sang.

The final rush was through the inner gate ; the tall massive wooden doors, bossed and studded with iron, had been blown inwards. One of them was still partly in position, and lay slanting downwards from the top, the other was blown almost to the ground. The deep circular archway of the gateway overhead made an ebony frame for the ivory moonlight picture within. We ran along the slanting door, and as I jumped from the end of it to the ground I almost jumped on top of a soldier who was in the act of skewering a Chinaman to the earth with his bayonet. He squirmed and wriggled like a worm as he received prod after prod. The corpses of many Chinamen lay around. A tumult of fighting had been here. From the gate-house above, where the Japs were engaged in a hand-to-hand encounter with the defenders, their progress could be followed by the cheering and rattling of musketry. Gradually it slackened, and finally ceased altogether. The great white street stretched up from the gate ; all the houses were roofless and in ruins as far as could be seen from where we stood. On the top of the wall itself lay the corpses of many Chinamen, and on the wooden floors of the gate-house were many, their blood making dark pools on the dusty boards. A badly-clad lot they looked, yet they had certainly defended that gate with great stubbornness and determination, as the Japanese loss amounted to 220 men.

When the Japanese had formed up along the wall they appeared to muster about a thousand men. Far ahead of us to the right, in the direction of the legations, a great fire was burning. We took it to be a beacon light, probably kindled to guide us to the relief of the besieged. The Japanese marched briskly on along the wall, which made, in fact, a very good well-paved road, with a loop-holed parapet on the outward side, and here and there embrasures with dummy cannon. There was an immense number of these solid castings in the shape of guns all the way along the wall. Thousands of long gingalls and piles of modern rifles were lying scattered around.

What a city of ruins it looked in the bright moonlight! On our right hand side there appeared to have been a great conflagration. There was hardly a roof left standing, and only the walls of the one-storied houses remained. On our left over the wall the waters of the moat shone in a white silvery band, and beyond, the level country stretched away as far as the eye could reach.

Tramp, tramp the iron-shod heels of the soldiers rang on the stony road, and every now and then their bugles sounded alternately from one part or another of the long line. Those far behind sounded like a silvery echo of those in front. A good effect those bugles had calling to each other in the clear moonlight air. Some way on we met a Russian picket on the wall and learned that the legations had been relieved at three o'clock that afternoon.

The sunlight of the following day showed us how desperate had been the straits of the besieged and how gallant had been the defence. The picture presented by pale ghostlike little children was perhaps the most pitiable of all. The women looked worn from anxiety, work and nursetending, Lady MacDonald, for instance, bathing the fever patients in the hospital while Sir Claude directed the military operations of the defence, in which he was so ably seconded by Colonel Shiba who commanded the Japanese.

An Unpleasant Choice.

The editors of this volume have conveyed a suggestion to me that I should write them an account of what I think the most interesting ten minutes of my experience as a war correspondent. It is not easy to comply with a demand like that. Looking backwards I am convinced that the pleasantest period I ever experienced was when I entered a ramshackle "Eetkammer" on the Durban-Pretoria Railway the morning I got out of Ladysmith after the siege, and sat down to the first reasonably decent meal for four solid months. But that incident lasted over ten minutes and I do not believe that the history of it would be half as interesting for others to read about as it was for me to experience.

Now had I been told to write about my most unpleasant ten minutes' experience, as I intend to do, I should have had no difficulty whatever in making a selection. There comes to my mind a space of almost exactly that duration. It often comes there. I dream about it yet sometimes and it supplied me with sensations that I have no sort of desire to renew. It happened during the somewhat halting progress of the misunderstanding between the United States and Spain with regard to the affairs of the Island of Cuba.

I had been knocking about the Havana Channel and the Carribean Sea with the American Fleet for a couple of months in a ninety-ton, top-heavy steam-pilot boat called the "Sommers N. Smith." That title had been given to the craft, I believe, for the purpose of conferring a limited amount of immortality upon the genius who designed her. Unfortunately for her reputation, the vessel turned turtle at the moment of launching and drowned several people. To remedy the lack of stability thus disagreeably manifested a quantity of steel rails had been laid along the ship's keel.

The dead weight prevented a renewal of the initial calamity, but it also converted the ship into a fairly steady going pendulum, which the least bit of a sea would set in motion.

Two months of unceasing wobble over the waves of the Carribean Sea, together with the unusually large and particularly lively assortment of rats and cockroaches carried by the "Sommers N. Smith," had made me very willing to join a detachment of American marines who were landing on the swampy shores of Guantanamo Bay, to secure that inlet as a coaling station for the American warships and incidentally to seize the Cuban end of the cable between Cuba and Hayti. The change was not greatly for the better, but it was agreeable as an improvement upon the "Sommers N. Smith." For a week or so we put up with the inconvenience of Spaniards sniping us from the chapparal scrub on the hills and I had begun to accustom myself to the mosquitos, landcrabs, sandfleas, variegated smells and other delights of a Cuban swamp in the rainy season, not to mention the Cuban insurgents, who were the biggest nuisance of all. There is one of the editors who will remember that delectable spot.

One blazing June day Dr. McGill, a friend of mine who was in medical charge of the American depot ship lying in the bay, sent me a note inviting me to dine and sleep on board.

"You had better come by the water boat that will put off about four o'clock," said the Doctor's note, "because we are sending all our boats up the Caimenera River with a landing party at sundown, and you cannot come later." The battleship "Texas" and the cruiser "Marblehead" were also in the bay, and they, too, were sending all their boats up the river to search for submarine mines, so there would be no means of communication between the shore and the depot ship during the evening. Shortly after four I found myself on board. As I stepped in through the cargo port that was open on the main deck, the Doctor met me and casually mentioned that the ship had 1700 tons of ammunition on board including some 200 tons of gun cotton for the dynamite cruiser "Vesuvius," whose pneumatic guns made the nights hideous throwing that explosive over the hills towards the fortifications of Santiago.

"It's a nice lively cargo," said my friend, as we picked our way through the serried rows of 12-inch filled shells that covered the deck. "We'd have a nice, cheerful time if a fire broke out while the boats are away. There is a fine teeming population of sharks with healthy appetites in these waters, and a swim ashore after dark would be a new sensation for you."

Well, I didn't have a swim ashore, but the Doctor's casual remark turned out a first class prophecy in every other respect. After enjoying a capital dinner, oblivious of the potential earthquakes in the hold beneath our feet, we turned in shortly before midnight, and went to sleep. I was dreaming that I was home again in peaceful England, far away from Spanish "snipers," mosquitos, landcrabs, Cubans and other tropical luxuries, when I was awakened by the last notes of a bugle. For the moment I thought I was on shore and I sat up. A bump against the bunk above me did three things all at the same moment. It recalled me to the fact that I was on board ship, it make me wide awake in an instant, and it knocked me flat on my back, with a thundering pain in the top of my head. A fraction of a second later the bugle rang out again, and—Heavens! the bugler was blowing "fire quarters" with all the strength of his lungs.

If ever a bugler put his whole soul and intelligence into a bugle it was that man. There was no mistaking the meaning of the sound. No fire drill that ever was held could inspire a tithe of the urgency and terror that the bugler put into that call. Again and again his clarion rang out, and jumping from my bunk in my pyjamas I dashed out on deck. A panting figure flew past me in the darkness and yelled as he flew: "Come on like hell; she's afire!" I followed his direction as nearly as I knew how, my brain crammed with the wildest emotions.

Would it be better, I thought, to risk the explosion, which I feared would follow the fire, or take my chance with the evil brutes whose ghastly shapes in scores were outlined by blue lambent fires in the phosphorescent waters round the ship? Ugh! the thought of the hungry sharks chilled my blood, and I resolved to stand by the ship while half a chance remained.

Better to risk the explosion than the hungry maws outside.

Following the sailor of the emphatic tongue, I raced along towards the scene of the outbreak. It was in the cook's galley, and when I reached it a torrent of liquid fire was pouring out of the doors and flowing along the deck. The cook had set about preparing hot coffee against the return of the boats. His fire did not burn up quickly enough to please him and he had sought to stimulate it by pouring petroleum on it out of a can. The fire ignited and exploded the oil, setting alight another can that was on the galley floor. In an instant the whole place was in flames. The blazing oil poured out of the doors and ran along the deck in streams of living fire.

More quickly almost than it takes to write about it the ready sailors had rigged a firehose, and the pulsing engines, their throttles open wide, were driving a two-inch stream of water into the flames. The blazing oil crackled and sputtered for a moment and then, horror of horrors! it floated, still flaming, on the surface of the stream, the water carrying it more rapidly than ever towards the stacks of shell and packed ammunition boxes on the deck. Never have I seen men toil as the swarming crew, officers and men hauled and lifted to get the explosives beyond the reach of the flames as the oil raced towards them. Frantic orders, emphasised by strenuous oaths, were given to turn off the hose and for some seconds we gazed helplessly at the paralysing scene.

Could the fire not be stopped? Must we be either blown to pieces, or devoured by the greedy sharks? There seemed no alternative and I watched the yellow licking flames creep onwards towards the piles of ammunition. There was one hope. Our engineer, as one inspired, shouted an order to "Man the ash hoist!" Frantic fingers, working for dear life's sake, rigged the shoot, and from the depths of the stokehole heaping baskets of ashes flew up. It was our last chance. With furious, but ordered haste the inert ashes were hurled across the track of the advancing flames. The burning oil soaked into the dust dry ash like a sponge and blazed yet higher. Yet it seemed that its speed was checked. Again and again the laden baskets flew up the hoist, and almost before one could realise it a dam had been built across the path of the flaming flood. Would there be enough ashes in the boiler room? A minute and it was clear that the fire could be confined to the space round the galley, yet another and the dead weight of ash began to smother the leaping flames ; five minutes and only the stinking reek of petroleum vapour was rising from a black, greasy mound. Then the hose was again turned on and the whole accursed mass was swept into the sea. We were saved.

"Thank God that is over and past!" was the fervent prayer that escaped our lips. Those of us who had nothing more to do went on deck and, as we leant over the rail in the calm of the tropic night for a breath of air, we watched the waters swirl and shine where, here and there, and there—in a score of places—twenty-foot sharks, their hungry sides aglow with phosphorescence, swam round about us. We shuddered as we watched and heaved again a sigh of thankfulness. Then we found time—and words—to say things about the cook.

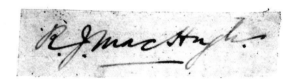

An Attempt that Failed.

After months of hard fighting and marching we drew near to Johannesburg. The army under Lord Roberts bivouaced on the veldt and day and night the crack of rifle and booming of cannon echoed among the hills that barred our way to the Golden City. We chafed at the delay, fearing that French's cavalry would be the first to enter. The temptation to push on was irresistible and Donohoe of " The Chronicle " and myself resolved to make the attempt. Eighteen miles of open country and the mines of the Black Reef lay between us and the foothills about Johannesburg.

Shadows were creeping across the plain when we mounted our horses. Avoiding the beaten track we struck into the dark heart of the veldt and moved swiftly and silently toward the hills. Six miles from camp the grass was on fire. Flame girdled the earth with a ruby zone and made the night intense. We kept touch with cry of the curlew. The rings of ruby closed about us and in our ears sang the roaring of fire and the crackling of the bush. We rode on till the chimneys of the Black Reef pointed gaunt fingers to the sky. Dismounting we led our horses along the edge of the reef and, tethering them to a tree, set out on foot toward the fires that flickered in the hills. Were they the bivouac fires of the enemy? That was the problem we had to solve. We crawled onward until dark shadows of men flitted about in the circles of light—Boer or British we could not tell. Closer and closer we crept through the stillness and blackness of the night. A man swinging a lantern approached and hailed a comrade in Dutch. We hugged the earth and held our breath ; then slowly and painfully wormed our way down the hill.

Convinced that General French must be threatening the enemy's line of retreat and that Johannesburg would be evacuated in a few hours, we renewed the attempt before the sun rose. Saddling fresh horses we **rode** out of camp accompanied by my servant, a half-caste who pleaded to be allowed to share our adventure. It was still dark when we answered the challenge of the sentry and passed beyond our lines—too dark to see that William was leading a second horse—my favourite. Presently we stumbled upon some horses picketed near a house and attended by a Kaffir who slept peacefully by their side. He swore that the animals were his master's and not those of a Boer patrol. At our bidding he threw open the door while we stood ready for a surprise. The house was empty. Emboldened by this proof that the enemy was not at hand we resumed our ride and in half an hour came in sight of a solitary store or "winkle," as it is called in South Africa.

"Come back!" cried Donohoe, who was a few paces behind. At the door of the winkle stood two men, one of them an armed Boer.

"If I do, they'll shoot," was my reply and we rode steadily on. The Boer disappeared and there remained a Jew who received us with manifest constraint.

"Any Boers about?" I asked.

"None," replied the store keeper.

"Where's the man you were speaking with just now?"

"I have neither seen nor spoken to a soul this morning except my wife;" and the fellow summoned his wife to support the lie.

Glancing beyond the gable end of the building I saw a Boer commando riding leisurely toward us.

"Who are they?" I asked, dropping my hand on the holster where my revolver lay. "Are they not Boers?"

The situation seemed hopeless. The enemy—two hundred or more in number—were already preparing to surround the store. Flight was impossible.

"We must be made prisoners," said Donohoe. "My horse would not have a ghost of a chance."

"There's no choice," I answered, and tried to console myself with the thought that good "copy" might come out of a siege of Pretoria.

Another peep at the cavalcade and my spirits rose with a bound. The Boers were still three or four hundred yards away and looked such peaceful, law abiding farmers. They were the last people in the world to require the services of a British newspaper correspondent. At the same time it was borne in upon me that I began the war in the siege of Ladysmith and ought not to end it in a siege of Pretoria. Moreover, if these gentlemen detained me I should miss the entry into Johannesburg. As I was not familiar with the Dutch taal it might be difficult to convince them how necessary it was for me to witness this historic event.

"I'm off," I cried. " I can't be any use here," and at the touch of the spur my horse sped like a bolt from the long bow. I strove to keep the store between me and pursuit.

"You're going right into them," shouted Donohoe, who stood near the gable watching the Boers stream round the building. There was nothing for it but the road and I took it on wings. William was not far behind, for he feared his former masters more than their rifles. The road dipped and gave us a few seconds' cover. Thrice I turned and looked back upon a prospect that seemed brighter every time, though the sunlit air hummed with the angry drone of wasps. The song of the bullet grew fainter and my heart was light once more. On and on we bounded until the thunder of pursuit almost died away and I felt that the danger was past. But a cry from my servant brought me up sharp. His horse staggered and rolled over—shot through the groin. Now I was glad of the led horse. William was on his feet and in the saddle like a streak of lightning. Ten minutes more and our self-respect began to return; we no longer felt like criminals fleeing from justice. Our horses fell into a gentle canter as we talked of the incident and cursed the unhappy store keeper.

"Halt!" The command rang out sharp and clear as the crack of a Mauser. I stopped dead and looked down the barrels of two rifles. A wild resolve seized me and I turned instinctively to the open veldt. But the cry of " Halt!" still rang in my startled ears and the rifles looked very near—so near that I felt the chill of steel on my wet brow. Pretoria might not be such a bad place after all, and there were correspondents enough to describe Lord Roberts' entry into Johannesburg. I looked again. "Are you Boers?" I exclaimed. "No," replied two men in dirty khaki and slouch hats. "We're Roberts' Scouts."

Five minutes later fifty troopers with Captain Mackenzie at their head were in wild chase of our pursuers and an hour afterward the advancing columns were smartly engaged in the neighbourhood of the store. A figure in khaki seated on a white horse riding off in the midst of a Boer commando was the last I saw of Donohoe until we entered Pretoria.

But before night fate frowned upon me. My horse fell into a prospecting hole, breaking two of my ribs and rupturing a muscle in my side. However, I entered Johannesburg on horseback two days later, and in a Cape cart witnessed the capture of Pretoria.

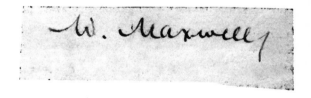

War's Mercies and War's Satires.

Of two officers whom I know well, F. was quiet and modest to a fault ; H. was fond of words and himself to a fault. The bearing of one made a heavy fire seem slight ; that of the other made a slight fire seem heavy. F. had led in many charges, but the bullet that cut an artery in his chest found him standing among a group of staff officers. " Is it bad ? " he asked softly of the surgeon in whose arms he rested. His ebbing strength, if not the surgeon's " Yes, pretty bad," warned him that the worst had come. " Tell my little wife God bless her and good-bye," he said. Now, H. was also struck in the chest—just after his line had scaled an enemy's trench, of course. With him, as with the other, the ruling instinct was strong. " It is fitting that I should die in battle," he said. " The H's have always been brave." A week later he was convalescent. This was in keeping with the eternal fitness of things, if you will. F. needed death to publish his virtues ; H. did not.

When General Anderson advanced on San Pedro Macati, one Filipino alone retreated in order. With a score of rifles blazing at him, he fell back by stages, kneeling and firing carefully. " He's too gallant to die ; let him go," said the General. When he had emptied his magazine he remained in the open; all his comrades had escaped into the bamboo. Instead of following them, he ran to the bank of the Pasig on which our left guarded. Deliberate in his calculations still, standing up as boldly as a hammer thrower, he threw his treasured Mauser far out into the stream. Then he jumped in and swam strongly toward the opposite bank. There was a crack from the end of the line. Some good shot, preoccupied with the game, had given sinister proof of his marksmanship. No one knew the name of the hero who sank. Probably his own family did not know how he died. This guileless little man, in all trust and courage and honesty, had practiced what he had learned at drill and what the agitators had preached. Sooner or later, death was bound to be the penalty of his ingenuousness. It came to him, at least, when he had an audience of brave men ; and in that, fate was merciful.

His humble preoccupation with the work in hand was of the same order as that in high places ; as that of a Lawton. Taller than any member of his staff and riding a taller horse than any of them, Lawton heightened his distinction with a huge white helmet. " It is the coolest helmet in the East ; it fits me like an old shoe," he said. Beside such considerations, the danger of being a mark was insignificant. When the fire was hot he would remove his treasure and revolve it slowly between his hands, the while he watched his line.

" You're safe as long as you twirl that helmet," I once suggested banteringly to him.

No one was quicker to give or to apprehend a joke ; but now he looked at me inquiringly. He did not know that he did twirl his helmet.

We reasoned that mathematical laws of chance made inevitable the death of one who exposed himself as constantly as did Lawton. We imagined him falling when, statuelike, he sat his horse in the heat of action. Of course, he was caught casually by a sniper's bullet. The mercy was that he died instantly and in harness, as he had always desired.

Apart with this same preoccupation which made Lawton unconsciously careless was that of the artillerist L. A correspondent came and stood beside the guns. " You'll get killed if you stay there," L. remarked calmly. The correspondent's sceptical laugh was cut by a Mauser bullet through the throat. L. looked up from his work for an instant. " I told you so," he said, and went on pumping shells into the enemy as coolly as if he were working out a problem in ballistics at Leavenworth.

You can never tell how action will affect a man. I have known one who was most excitable over an overdone steak or a missing piece of baggage to be as cold as ice in battle. I have known one who could bluff with unchanging face in a no-limit poker game to lose his head completely at the sound of a bullet. In a week in the rough life of camp or in five minutes in action you may get the epitome of human character. The march to the relief of Peking was a scalpel that laid quivering muscles and twitching nerves bare. On the hardest day of all, when, unless moved by the gasping intake of weary lungs, the powder from the tall kowliang and the particles of dust fell straight as dead weights to the ground, I was with the American contingent which lay panting on the road in an interval of rest. I saw one private in his agony out of sheer malignity turn and strike a comrade who was too worn and dispirited to resent the blow. Almost in the same moment I overheard another man whisper to his "bunky:" "I've got a little water in my canteen. You need it more than I do, Jim." Those drops were both the milk and the champagne of human kindness.

Often great courage amounts to a kind of high hysteria, which, in its extreme, has the effect of calm. Two dying men were lying beside each other one night in the Philippines. "Well, we might as well whistle as be sad," one said. "Sure!" the other answered. So they made the effort which gave their spirits strong flight; which made death more terrible to those who looked on than to those who died.

My own choice of heroes may be captious. That comedy-tragedy in which the Greeks mistook a memory for a strain of heredity gave me two, an official telegrapher and a shepherd, which I shall always cherish as an antidote to selfishness and pretense.

The telegrapher was a dry, wrinkled, little old man who spoke many languages (doubtless learned in a garret) so modestly that, instead of compliments, he seemed to court criticism for not knowing more. Once at Larissa, when the clamoring correspondents berated him because he could not make one wire carry all theirs as well as the official dispatches, some good angel prompted me to smile on him and to sympathize with him as the hardest-worked man in the Peninsula. So we became friends. I saw more than his straight nose. I saw something in his character suggesting the days when Greece had both philosophers and soldiers. One day, while he was busy under shell fire, I asked him if he did not mind the danger.

"Mind the danger!" he said. "I have my duty. When I take up

a new message I hear these noises ; but I am too busy to look out and see."

If the disputants of the army of the café which marched out and ran back again had done their day's work as well as he or the old shepherd, the world might still believe that blood will tell through two thousand years— which signalizes the survival of a poetic tongue.

I saw the shepherd only twice. The first time was in the crisis of the battle of Domoko. Back of the Greek guns, in the range of all the shells that passed over the ridges where they were placed, I noticed, in a moment when I lifted my eyes from the spectacle beyond, my hero in homespun driving his flock toward the rear. He, too, had no time to look out and see. He was as intense with the business in hand as a speculator who sees his fortune rise and fall with the quotations of the stock ticker. A bursting shell hid him in dust, but he reappeared and brought his scattered ewes together. The great game of the battle was forgotten. No matter how many soldiers fell, I had eyes only for him till he and his property were out of danger.

The next morning, when Homer's sun rose on the chaos of retreat gorging the pass from Domoko to Lamia, I saw the shepherd again. He was carrying a lamb under either arm. The Irregulars had taken the rest. In their mercy they may have listened to his plea that he might keep the ancestors of a new flock.

Later, in Lamia, I overheard a staff officer scolding the breakfastless, dinnerless, supperless little old telegrapher. I knew this officer well. In the days of mobilization he had boasted that he would kill a hundred Turks with his own hand ; but when the war came and the old fear of their masters gripped the subject race of yesterday, he had shown that he was afraid of fire.

" It has been a grand downfall," he said gaily, as if that were something to be proud of.

" It has illustrated the diversity of human nature and the helplessness of lambs," I thought.

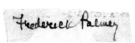

The War and the Walker.

A small, condensed war was fought in the southeastern corner of Europe seven years ago. It was fought and finished in less time than the Campaign of the Imperial Hotel has occupied. This was annoying, especially to correspondents who missed steamer connections and to one of the military attaches, whose new uniform was not finished before the treaty of peace was signed.

The principal annoyance, however, was the great regularity of the retreats indulged in by the lesser combatant. Its army was never too fatigued to fall back. A penchant for night retirements, coupled with cheerful disregard for tired correspondents who joined these inglorious processions, made the plains of Thessaly anything but a pleasure resort for the chroniclers of events.

It was this state of affairs which resulted in my remarkable record as a pedestrian. In the walking match from Domokos to Molos, by way of Furka Pass, Lamia and Thermopolyae, I was easily amongst the first. A number of others also walked and a few envious persons are inclined to dispute my claims for a medal. I may as well tell you, however, that my chief critic, who wrote and retreated for a Copenhagen paper—I forget his name but remember his beard—was deficient in the matter of legs. He had the full number but they were not as long as some others I might mention.

I feel that I am entitled to a medal for the Domokos-Molos go-as-you-please event. If His Hellenic Majesty takes any interest in athletics he will consider my case.

The Greeks sat down at Domokos after the usual hurried excursion southward—this time from Pharsala—to take breath and to think things over. The industrious army of Edhem Pasha, following the same trail, also sat down and declared a well earned holiday.

We, in Domokos, could see the white tented city of the enemy, far to the left across the plain. The enemy attended strictly to the Feast of Ramadan, however, and gave no heed to the Greeks in the hills. Meanwhile we mended our boots and made inquiries as to the state of the roads in our rear.

One bright morning,—May seventeenth—the Turks finished their Bank Holiday diversions and resumed the pleasures of the chase. We saw them from the hilltop trenches above Domokos, leisurely spreading across the green plain,—horse, foot and guns, and methodically firing each deserted village as they advanced.

The ball opened at high noon and continued until moonrise. The Greeks fought well. It was a very spectacular performance and from our seats in the gallery we had a splendid panorama spread before us.

I photographed freely and at nightfall went back into the town to snatch a few hours, sleep before the battle was resumed. The Greeks were bringing in their wounded. Everyone was in high spirits. The various disasters that would befall the Infidel foe on the morrow were detailed to me with a great relish by an infantry captain as we threaded our way through the steep, slippery streets of the old town.

His recital was interrupted by the discovery that more trouble confronted us. A line of burning villages reddened the neighboring hills in our rear, announcing the presence of the inevitable flanking party. It was very sad and altogether wrong but nothing was apparently left but another retreat.

About midnight a miscellaneous collection of soldiers, artillery, peasants, live stock and Red Cross vehicles rolled across the plain behind Domokos. It was a sullen march. Viewed from the foot hills it suggested a nightmare. There were sheep and goats driven by weary herders, women and children huddled on horses and donkeys, wounded soldiers who swore or wept, savage officers and camp followers with an eye to loot.

Our departure from Domokos was unceremonious and I found that my horse had been mislaid. It seemed a waste of time to stop and look for him when there was such good company on the march. The matter was hardly worth debating. I fell into line, equipped with some exposed photographic films, a large appetite and the desire to walk rapidly.

I did walk rapidly. I passed regiments of infantry attempting to maintain a semblance of marching order—and left them in the rear. I came up with some fragments of cavalry and dodged around them and left them in the rear. I dimly remember passing long lines of rough two-wheeled carts, filled with groaning men, and—leaving them in the rear—I took short cuts through and around the mob and crossed the plain, directly behind Domokos with winged feet. Never did man walk so energetically or so tirelessly.

I hit the foothills joyously and went up a steep slope without stopping. The wagon road was winding and irregular. I took the direct route—an acute angled goat path. Why waste time? I remember so well how I looked back—from the top of the hill—and seeing the straggling column in the moonlight below and thinking to myself that it would detain the advancing Turks for at least a few minutes. I could do wonders in those few minutes.

I remember passing two red shirted Garibaldians—one of them wounded in the shoulder—lying a few feet from the roadway. They knew no English and I no Italian but we agreed without difficulty that the cause of the excitement was " la toork." Water I had none and the wounded Garibaldians lay down again with a groan. I passed into the night, outstripping a herd of goats and heading generally for Lamia, which I dimly remembered to be a town with restaurants and beefsteaks and a well of cool water.

I passed a simple peasant lad with his possessions on a donkey cart. He had sold me fresh mutton in Domokos. He looked honest. I gave him my overcoat to carry as far as Lamia. An overcoat hampers a record making pedestrian. I was to see him at Lamia, beside the well in the public square and there receive my overcoat and the two precious rolls of photographic films—pictures of the battle—which it contained. Alas !

I struck the main road again and made better time. The army was now miles behind. Every time I turned a fresh corner, I received a pleasant surprise. Not a Turk was to be seen.

At sunrise I sat down on a boulder by the roadside. I was not tired, but I wanted to give the competing army a fair chance. John Bass skidded by on an American bicycle, heading for Watras.

He flashed a greeting and was gone. He disturbed me. It was not right that the End of the World, the Finish of All Things, should be participated in by a man on a bicycle.

I continued towards Lamia. I have reason to believe that I was the first refugee in the town, for there were still beefsteaks and fresh water. Never have I eaten such beefsteaks, revile them though I had, two weeks before.

I sat under a tree that day and reviewed the army and the goats as they filtered through the public square. Some of the army had been quarantined at Furka Pass that morning in a futile attempt to bring order out of chaos. But many of the soldiers broke quarantine and reached Lamia. So did he peasants—all but my simple goatherd with my rolls of Kodak films and overcoat.

By dusk that evening I had seen enough wounded men and dust covered stragglers to populate a city. I began to think seriously of a hotel bed, with sheets and pillows. But about nine o'clock word came that the army had not done retreating. The occupants of Lamia forthwith joined the procession and we crossed another interminable plain, steering for Thermopolyae. Captain Dorst, the American military attache, who was searching for the Greek army, accompanied me.

I continued through the night without hunger or fatigue, walking steadily. At seven in the morning we reached Molos, where the village schoolmaster played the Good Samaritan. I slept for a day and a night in the military telegraph office and when I woke up the war was over.

I should like to know if those films were a success. The overcoat, I contribute cheerfully to the reconstruction of Thessaly.

Adrift on an Ice-Pack.

" Battle, murder and sudden death " are presumably the subjects best adapted to a sketch of the type demanded by the editors of this enlightened volume. My experience of the first lies in the future, across the islet-studded Korean Straits ; the second I have not yet committed, though if the Japanese War Office keeps me anchored in Tokyo much longer my hands will indubitably be stained by Secretarial gore ; the last it has been my luck to baffle narrowly on one or two occasions. Perhaps the reader would like to hear about one such incident.

The experience descended upon me in February, 1901. I was on my way to Peking to put an end to the Boxer disturbance which had assumed dimensions sufficient to justify the presence of a person of my importance. Of course the Gulf of Liautong was gripped in the icy fingers of winter, a shield of ice fending off the daring steamer which designed to achieve any of the Gulf ports. Ching-wan-tao was my objective and a miserable little 80 horse-power tank called the *Kwang-chi* had the felicity of being entrusted with the task of bearing me to my destination. The sea was as clear of ice as the writer's conscience of evil when we left Chefoo. But when we got fairly into the Gulf we struck it. It was delusively thin at first. The steamer's bows went through it with as much ease as a knife through cheese, and the grating scrunch, sc-r-r-unch, supplied a pleasing change from the monotonous splash of the waves as they erstwhile broke against the sides of our vessel. This lasted for about a couple of hours. Then the ice changed from the down on the peach, so to speak, to the skin. It became two, three, even four inches thick. The poor little *Kwang-chi* had evidently no ambition to go into business as an ice-smasher. Whenever a particularly heavy patch was struck, she shivered all over and stopped dead. The engines then had to be reversed, and after going astern for fifty or sixty yards, the order "full steam ahead" would be given from the bridge, and she would courageously charge into the thick of the pack, generally with the result of getting forward fully fifty yards before she was again "hung up." This hilarious method of progression continued until we were about 15 miles east of Ching-wan-tao, when we got finally and effectively blocked. The captain, who had been in a state of apprehension throughout lest he should buckle his bow-plates or do some other of those things which might with more than equal advantage be left undone, announced his intention of returning to Chefoo. Lieutenant Mahon, R.E., one of the passengers, and I, upon learning that this determination had been arrived at, decided to walk ashore across the ice. Mahon had come out from India in connection with the railway work which had been taken in hand by the China Expeditionary Force (of course the war was still dragging along at that time), and he was naturally anxious to report himself at Shan-hai-kuan as soon as possible. His anxiety to see the dust of North China on his feet was only equalled by mine. Some waggish person on board said we were only five miles from the shore, and this recklessly mendacious assertion was supported by others who purported to know something about it.

Of course we were a pair of unmitigated idiots to attempt to walk ashore—but we had scarcely either of us attained half-way to the golden mean of life. So, in a breezy and cocksure way, we told the other passengers that we would send out coolies to bring them and our baggage ashore, nodded a jaunty farewell and set out feeling as pleased with ourselves as does a correspondent who imagines he has beaten the censor. Mahon had skates; hadn't. This led to trouble. We were tied together, following the advice of a Swedish second officer, who reckoned he knew something about the dark ways and vain tricks of ice. Mahon went off at a ten second bat, with the immediate result that I pitched on my nose while he whacked the ice with the back of his head as if he meant it. He swore at me, but when I opened the flood gates of my eloquence—an Australian has little to learn in this species of linguistic accomplishment—he cordially acknowledged that he was over-matched and we started a trifle more warily.

We went on for about three hours, occasionally happening upon thin ice but without meeting further trouble. The shore however did not seem to come any nearer. It remained as distant as Alexieff's fleet from the brunt of battle. Then the fun started. We found the ice was getting thinner. After going for another hour or so we found that there was a couple of miles of open water between us and the shore. At this stage Mahon also found open water. He slipped through. It was a bit of a job getting him out too. However, it was accomplished. I sought expectantly in my pocket for a brandy flask which I had placed there. It was empty, a small hole at the bottom telling its own sad tale. Mahon's language warmed the whole atmosphere. Then I slipped through. Mahon yanked me out and from that on we busied ourselves chiefly in falling through and hauling each other out. It was a monotonous occupation. We determined to go back to the *Kwang-chi* and face the fleers and sneers of our fellow passengers. Night had fallen them and it was as cold as woman's charity for woman. The steamer we found had left. We spent a cheerful night on the back, a cold wind, blowing straight from the North Pole, encouraging us to sprawl about the slippery ice as rapidly as circumstances permitted in a vain effort to keep our blood circulating. The night passed in some way and in the morning we recommenced falling through the ice and dragging each other out again. Really, this method of amusement, through undoubtedly novel, quickly palled on one. How were we rescued? We rescued ourselves. Away to the south a promontory (Pei-ta-ho) jutted abruptly and aggresively into the ice-bound sea. We made for it. The thrilling adventures we had on the way were of consuming interest—to us— but I will not inflict a recital of them upon the jaded reader. We arrived opposite Pei-ta-ho, miserable, hungry, thirsty, despondent. A channel of water about 40 yards wide separated us from a stretch about 100 yards broad of firm ice on the other side of which lay the shore—and safety. Mahon wanted to swim. In an uninterested, mechanical, listless kind of way I explained that such a course meant summary suicide.   He retorted that that was better than dying by inches. There appeared to be some horse-sense in that, so I did not continue the argument.   Pieces of small ice floated by.   Suddenly a big piece grounded at our feet, swung round, jammed against the other side and so made a bridge—to life. We sprinted across and (almost as in the case of two other illustrious persons, Spurious Lartius and Herminius, in connection with the bridge over the Tiber) as we reached the other side it floated off.   We were safe.   A Chinese Joss-Pidgin man did very well at Pei-ta-ho and the 24th Punjaub Infantry sent out a medical detail to salvage us from his well-meant but ill-directed attentions.   We had been 25 hours on the ice-pack.

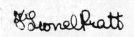

An Adventure in Bulgaria.

It was during the Russo-Turkish War that the little incident which I have endeavoured to illustrate took place. I had followed for some six months the fortunes of the Turkish troops and had been present at many a hard fought battle. The army under the command of Nedjib Pasha was encamped waiting for further instructions from Constantinople. Close to the camp was a Bulgarian village and my colleagues of the press, among them Coningsby of the " Times," Drew Gay, of the " Daily Telegraph," Huyshe, and many others very soon came to the conclusion that a room in a house was far superior to a tent, more particularly as it was pouring rain most of the time. So all of us proceeded to the village with our horses, carts and baggage and very soon found most comfortable quarters. The houseowner with whom I made arrangements was a Bulgarian, and anything but prepossessing to look at. But all I cared about was shelter. The man gave me a stable for my horses and a very large room for me to work and sleep in. I set my camp bed up in a corner away from the door and made myself as comfortable as possible. Coningsby and Drew Gay were in a house close by. Sometimes they called on me and sometimes I went across to them for a chat. Our commissariat was not at all bad, as we could buy chickens and geese for a few piastres—one piastre being worth about two pence halfpenny--and my host used to supply me with potatoes, eggs and milk. The latter he used to send up to my room by his daughter, who, by the way, was an exceedingly pretty girl of about thirteen. She had been in my room on many occasions and I had had many interesting conversations with her through the aid of my interpreter. And now comes the point of my story. I had been making a sketch of her to introduce into a drawing I was at work on. She was leaving the room after a sitting and I thoughtlessly chuckled her under the chin and told her she was a very pretty child. She laughed and ran downstairs and, naturally, told her father. He, apparently, did not regard the little familiarity as innocently as I did for he flew into a towering rage and swore he would be revenged for what he called the insult. Luckily my trusted servant heard the threats that the man made and came at once and warned me. The poor fellow was evidently seriously alarmed; his hair almost stood on end and his eyes bulged in his head as he entered my room. With intense earnestness and excitement he whispered to me what the wrathful father had said, how he had declared that I had insulted his daughter and tried to lure her away from him and that he would have my life for it. I should explain that at that time the Bulgarians hated the English, who were then very friendly towards the Turks. I laughed at the whole story but this only made my servant the more anxious, and he begged me to leave the house and go back to camp. I pooh-poohed that as ridiculous; but as my man was evidently filled with genuine anxiety for my safety I told him that I would be very careful and that as an additional precaution he was to sleep in my room while one of my Circassians would sleep just outside the door, while another would sleep in the stable lest my murderous host should take it into his head to injure my horses or let them loose.

I should explain that all the doors and windows of the house and all the wood that could be easily removed had been carried away by the troops for firewood so that I was therefore unable to make my room secure in any way. As night came on I confess that my servant's fears communicated themselves to me in some measure and I felt just a little nervous as to what might happen if what my man had told me was true. So I took the precaution, when going to bed, of placing my revolver under my pillow. There is no doubt but that I owe my life to this fact. Previous to retiring I visited the stables and found my horses all right with my faithful Circassian, Isack, on guard, his Winchester repeating rifle by his side. My other Circassian was lying on the floor outside my door and my brave servant, Yanco, was asleep just inside the doorway. I got into bed with a vague feeling of danger. I soon found that it was one thing to go to bed but that it was another to fall asleep. I tried not to think about the affai and rolled from side to side determined that I should go to sleep. But it was no use; one eye would close but the other would be wide awake. The light from a full moon was streaming in through my open window and I had just turned my face to the room when a strange sound struck upon my ear.

To my horror I saw the figure of a man moving slowly towards my bed. He had evidently stepped across the sleeping forms of my men and to avoid waking them was stealthily creeping along the floor. I could see the moonlight shining on the cold steel of the yataghan he clutched in his hand. I could see as plainly as in the daylight the absolutely fiendish expression of the man's face and I realised that it was a duel to the death between him and me. My nerves were at their utmost tension but I waited until he was only a few feet away from my bed, then suddenly drawing my revolver, which I had ready in my hand, I fired. The man started but I could see that I had missed him. He turned on the instant and made a dash towards the window. As he turned I fired again but my haste and excitement were too much and I missed him again, the bullet going very wide of its mark. My enemy in his surprise and his haste to get out of the room dropped his yataghan and I have it at home now among my curios.

By this time my servant and Circassian had joined in the excitement and we three were firing at the Bulgarian as he jumped out of the window on to a verandah, then racing down some steps into the courtyard tore down the street. How it happened I do not know but there is one thing certain, my two Circassians and my servant with Winchester repeating rifles and I with a service revolver fired some 15 shots, and we all failed in bringing down the man.

It now occurred to me that this incident had assumed a serious aspect. What was I to do? To remain there was impossible, for he m'ght return at any moment reinforced with his friends and give me a bad time, I therefore sent one of my Circassians with a hastily written note to my General, Nedji Pasha, informing him of what had taken place and asking what I should do in the matter.

While waiting for the reply my servant rushed into the house as I kept guard, and packing my baggage as quickly as possible brought it outside. He had just finished when my messenger arrived with the information that the General was sending me twenty-five soldiers for protection and that I was to burn the house and return to camp.

I often have owned to myself when thinking over my action that perhaps I was a little hasty ; but in those days it seemed different, for I simply had my goods placed in a cart, my horses brought out from the stables and then calling out the wife and children I set fire to the house with my own hands, and by the time my Turkish guard arrived on the scene, the house was a roaring mass of flame. There was one thing I had overlooked in my ferocious revenge and that was I very nearly included my two campaigning friends and their goods in the bonfire, for I had not calculated how close their house was to mine. It escaped, however, and so did my would be assassin, for on my return to camp I learned we were to march the next day.

Taking It Lying Down.

Under ordinary circumstances, when a man calls you a liar there is only one thing to be done. He may say you prevaricate, or that he does not believe you; all the same he has called you a liar, and a certain series of results usually follow. Now the offense of telling another man in all seriousness that he lies is a great one; in fact, it is charging him with breaking one of the ten commandments (which is a very bad thing to do) and should be resented. However that may be, the general law that circumstances alter cases is well known in this present age, and in that particular part of this age when General Buller was campaigning in Natal enough circumstances arose to alter a great many cases.

On the second day of the battle of Vaal Krantz two of us rode out to the advance post of the British position. The other man was Knox, of Reuter's agency. This advance position was being held by one brigade of infantry, the battle at that period consisting chiefly of an artillery duel on the right flank. Everything seemed to be fairly quiet as we approached, and not once were we halted on the suspicion of being Boer spies. The blue coat I wore generally brought about such an arrest on almost every excursion we undertook, but we had grown accustomed to that by this time, nor did we pay any particular attention to the omission on this occasion; and yet that blue coat in the end proved to be at the bottom of the trouble, and it was a very good coat, too, by the way.

We had only just begun to interview one of the colonels of the reserve forces when suddenly a heavy fusilade broke out somewhere near, and a whirring sounded in the air like the blast of a strange kind of wind. Then a big tin biscuit can got up by itself and went clattering down the hillside over the stones. A voice from the crest above us shouted: " Stand, boys, stand! " in a curiously insistent monotone.

The hillside leapt into life. The Colonel bellowed orders ; the reserve troops lifted up from the ground like the startled gasp of a man surprised, and bending low to the rocks went hurrying in disorder toward the crest.

It happened to be Knox's turn to hold the horses. In the shelter behind the kraal an unarmed orderly also gave his horses to Knox, and taking the rifle and cartridge belt from a soldier previously wounded, who was lying there, he ran around the kraal in the direction of the firing ; and in the nature of things I followed the orderly. By taking a circuitous route we kept below the range of fire for the first half of the distance. Then we began the ascent, the orderly some fifteen yards ahead, leaping from one sun-bleached rock to another, and waving his rifle wildly as his balance swayed from side to side.

When we reached the left wing of the firing line held by a Scotch regiment, the fight was cracking fiercely all along the rocky crest. The attack of the Boers had been brought to a standstill not more than 400 yards away, and it seemed at that time to be a question of nip and tuck if they would be able to come on again or not. The British were firing at random from behind whatever cover there was at hand. Here a rock sheltered three of them, there two more lay protected. The line zigzagged back and forth because at this end no regular trench had been constructed. Some of them were shooting over their comrades' heads. Among the men there were shouts and curses and deep-drawn groans, and the silence of a number of dead already.

My rock—we had come to look upon them as though we owned them, like dwellings, and I had picked out the finest one in the near neighborhood —my rock, then, was situated about 20 yards from a dead white stump of a tree, the only one on the hill. Beside this stump a soldier knelt on one knee.

As in all times of excitement such as this was the attention is apt to become fastened upon a certain part of the whole, so in this case my interest in the battle became centered in watching this man. I could see his face plainly. It was a strange face ; a face that could be turned from a demon's to a clown's by a smile. For a while he stared intently straight ahead

Then he slowly lifted his rifle without shifting his gaze, as though instead of laying his eye to the sights he was raising the sights to his eye. He fired, and the unholy savage joy which overspread the countenance of that clown face was wonderful.

I had grown so absorbed in watching this performance that I had paid no heed to the extra amount of shouting around me, but after the clown had " got his man " I became aware of considerable commotion in our part of the line. At this time the attack of the enemy was redoubled, as though the Boers were making a last determined effort to carry the crest. Above the increasing crash of the battle I could not distinguish what was said, but there was something out of the way for a certainty.

Then a young Scotch soldier, his blue eyes bright with the light of battle, his tunic torn across the chest, and his rifle firmly gripped in one hand, came running toward me by sections, darting from shelter to shelter. Finally he reached the last stage of his journey and throwing himself down at full length beside me, he glared at me fiercely. There was barely room for both of us lying flat.

" Wha air ye ? " he asked in an angry tone.

My telling him I had no intention of sitting up from the shelter just then in order to show him my papers seemed to strike him as reasonable.

" Wha air ye ? " he repeated, somewhat mollified.

" A war correspondent."

" Laddie, A dinna believe ye," he said solemnly.

And there it was. In plain English, at least plain enough, and in all seriousness to be sure, he had called me a liar to my face. But this was one of those cases altered by circumstances.

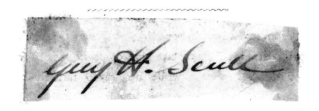

Without Orders.

I fancy this volume will teem with South African experiences, but what can one write otherwise, when one's most adventurous incidents all occurred there, with the stern reminder ever before him that it must be his most thrilling adventure.

I forget the date, but it does not matter. It was just after the siege of Wepener, in April, 1900. At that time I was in charge of a troop of irregular mounted infantry. My column marched due north from Wepener to Thaba 'nchu and from there due east eight miles, and when a halt was called about ten miles west of Ladybrand, things happened. As General Campbell's column was operating on our extreme right we consequently thought that when we got so near Ladybrand his brigade had occupied the town. On this assumption I acted. As president of our mess, and as one of the many liking a drop of the " cratur," it occurred to me that my column must get a look in as regards the supply of the cheery article, not wishing to leave it all to our successors. Accordingly I sent two men with duly certified passes to buy, beg or steal stuffing for saddles (sic); in reality, to buy as much of the necessities of life as were left in the town. The result threatened to be disastrous, as future events will show. The two men—I should mention that they were Americans of the cowboy breed, whom I had recruited from mule ships at East London—started about half an hour after " outspanning." On leaving the camp myself about half an hour before " skimmel," riding, dreamily tripping, forgetful of all surroundings, forgetful even of my men ahead and of the country swarming with the enemy, lights loomed to right and left of me, and I was pulled up sharply with the deadly " Wij loop da?" Then I realised the town was reached. Instantly Boers, fully armed, sprang out of nothingness around me ! What was to be done ? I was for scooting, but probably if I did so I would be shot. Had

I better not try a bluff? I was very undecided, but the thought of the two men whom I had ordered in front stayed me. Seeing an hotel before me on which floated the Vierkleur I rode quietly up to it, instantly dismounted, and called a nigger in a lordly manner to hold my horse. I demanded a bottle of champagne and an exchange of flags. Although quaking in my shoes, the change was effected in twenty minutes. How glad I was once more to find myself beneath a bit of the old bunting. I entered the bar and found my two troopers very drunk, but nevertheless, as I afterwards discovered, very sensible. Undoubtedly I owe to them my fortunate escape from a very awkward quandary. On entering I accosted them as follows :

" Well, what's to be done? We're in a hole."

" See here, Lieutenant," one replied, " I guess you'd better leave that to us."

I went on drinking, what was my first indulgence for many moons, quietly awaiting developments. The troopers went out, and evidently had spun a red hot yarn, for when they condescended to call me, they were sitting at the Mayor's desk in the Town Hall, issuing instructions to all and sundry, that on surrendering they must confine themselves to their houses indefinitely, under penalty of being shot. The passes were signed by a saddler, Sergt.-Major !

Heaven knows what they thought your humble servant must have been. However, all's well that ends well, and when all were safely housed, and when we had taken 320 surrenders, and 190 rifles, of which about one hundred were Martinis, which we promptly destroyed, and about seventy Mausers, which we took into camp, we left town somewhat hurriedly. We arrived in camp about an hour before reveillé. Strange to relate, the column did not pursue its course into Ladybrand next day, but trekked back to Thaba 'nchu. However, the reasons were afterwards explained, and were that the general staff had the intention of driving the Boers wandering in the district into the town, and of afterwards surrounding it. I may mention that the next appearance of British troops in Ladybrand was when Col. Pilcher darted in with a hundred men and seized the Mayor, on which occasion he met with stern resistance and, I believe, with considerable

loss. In after days, at the time of Prinsloo's surrender, many of my
" prisoners " were captured, and I conversed with several of them, but they
never forgave me, and to them I am, and fear always will be, a veritable
" verdomde rooinek."

A Message from Andree.

Victoria, B. C., is a journalistic outpost and I have had many interesting experiences there. One week—it was during that rush to the Klondike's goldfields—was full of experiences. The coming of Mr. Tilton, mate of the whaler Belvedere, who had walked across Alaska from Point Barrow and taken passage south from Valdes on the little steam schooner Albion, started the week's excitement. He brought news of how five whaling steamers had been crushed in the ice of the Arctic, and of how the whaler Narwhal had been burned at sea and her men rescued from icefloes in the northern ocean. I caught him by chartering a small tug and taking her out to lie in the steamer's track. It was about nightfall when I sighted the Albion, and, with much signalling, managed to get the vessel's master to stop her long enough to allow me to hear a tale of shipwreck and disaster, which, when telegraphed to the several newspapers whose correspondent I was, made some front pages look beautiful from a correspondent's point of view. But it is not of this that I would tell, nor of that horror of the Dyea trail when the snow and ice slid down the Chilkoot Pass two days later and blotted out the lives of over one hundred and fifty men who had gone north to seek wealth, though I had no small amount of trouble, and incidental experiences, in getting this news to the nearest wire, the Victoria wires being at the time out of repair because of a gale.

This is to tell of another incident of that week, of a message from Andree—whom you may have forgotten, for fame's laurels oft fade quickly from the brow. As you may remember, Herr Andree was an intrepid aeronaut, who, in common with two other brave Swedish balloonists, set out from Sweden not many years ago in the balloon Eagle to seek the North Pole, and, like others, the trio lost their lives in the attempt. No one has learned their fate. For myself, I believe that the Eagle fell in the barren lands north of Fort Churchill on Hudson's Bay and Herr Andree and those with him were killed by the Esquimaux. There is no positive proof of this; nothing more than stories that have come from time to time from the natives of that vicinity stating that three men came from the air in a thing that looked like a great "omiak," or canoe, and the natives came from their igloos and killed them with bows and arrows.

Yet, all this does not concern my experience. It started with a telegram which I received one wintry morning as I sat at my desk in the office of the Victoria *Colonist*. This message was from one Rosenburg, a fur-buyer, who had come from Dawson City on the steamer Centennial. It was dated from Nanaimo, where the steamer had stopped to coal, and read :

"Meet Centennial. Due daylight. Jack Carr, mail carrier a board, has message letter found Andree pigeon."

I read this message with increasing excitement, for it told of a "story" in which the world would be interested. It was the "story" of the year. As I jammed the telegram in my pocket I began to think of plan after plan for landing this news all by myself. If I could get a "beat" on this it would be a big thing. But how?—that was the question.

Although I did not know the fact at that time, a rival correspondent had a similar telegram in his pocket, and he was thinking, as I did, of how he could keep the story "exclusive." In this effort he had chartered the tug Mystery and gone off into the stormy night, sea-sick but happy in the belief that he was alone with the story of the year. As for me, I roused agents and tugboat captains from their beds, spending the greater part of a wild night in going in a cab from house to house for this purpose ; but I could get no tug. All I could get was the knowledge that my rival had gone—which was not pleasant knowledge.

There was nothing for me to do but to wait. I went to the steamer's wharf, and sat on the piles there in the rain and wind, waiting, and shivering as I waited, for the arrival of the steamer. In the meantime, messengers brought to me answers to telegrams that I had sent. One was from Mr Martin. He was news editor of the New York *Herald*, and he instructed me as follows : " If Andree letter genuine try buy exclusively. Offer up to two thousand dollars, but be sure genuine." Then came another. It was from Mr. Johnson, of the San Francisco *Call*, who said.

"Will pay up to three thousand for Andree letter if Carr vouches verification. Insist this. We don't want buy gold brick."

And so said others. Not in those words, but in words that meant the same thing. They all wanted the news and were willing to pay for it, if Carr would vouch for it ; and with my pocket filled with flimsy I was waiting for Mr. Carr. It was nearly daylight when the Centennial came to the dock. My rival's tug was steaming almost alongside, and I noticed that one of her boats was smashed, while two of the Centennial's port boats were also stove in. I afterward learned that my rival's tug had bumped against the steamer in the night, and, after much swearing on the part of Capt. Thompson of the steamer, he had given his cheque in payment for the damage done.

How impatiently I waited for that steamer to make fast her lines, and how disgusted I was when I saw other correspondents emerge from their shelters and prepare to clamber over the rail with me. I can remember the whole thing very plainly. We clambered over the rail despite the protests of the crew and the swearing of the captain, and we invaded the cabin in which the mail carrier was closeted with Mr. Gibbons, my rival.

The mail carrier sat on a trunk. His feet were encased in the furlined "mukluks" of the northland and his mackinaw coat was thrown open carelessly, exposing a frayed red jersey. He was a typical mail carrier of the Klondike district of that day. But, as I remember well, I didn't pay much attention to his garb, for I was worrying more about my rival, and it was at him that I looked the most. It did not take long, though, to see by his manner that he had not been successful, and I began my work, as did the others who came with me.

Yes, the mail carrier said, he had a letter from Andree, but he considered it was worth a few hundred dollars to him. The papers would be glad to have it, he thought.

I offered him five hundred dollars for it, and he looked at me, as though he would have liked to have bargained with me, but my rival offered six hundred, and one of the other fellows—I think it was George Denny, now war correspondent for the Associated Press—made a bid. As I thought I had a good margin to bid on I offered a thousand dollars. My rival had seemingly as much money to offer as I had, though, for he at once offered two thousand, and the others disgustedly dropped out of the bidding. The more we bid and bargained, the more serious became the mail carrier. He scratched his head and wrinkled his brow, seemingly thinking deeply, and, after some minutes of silence, he said : "If you fellows'll wait, I'll talk to my friend about this thing. He's got a half interest." And we waited.

Hour after hour we waited, and then I bethought me of a scheme. My friend, Mr. W. A. Ward, was the consul of the Scandinavian government. Why couldn't he insist on the mail carrier giving up the letter ? It was worth trying, I thought, so I telephoned to Mr. Ward and he came quickly in a cab. But his interview with the mail carrier was ineffective. It had only the effect of making the man who walked across several thousand miles of ice very angry.

"I suppose you guys think you'll work me that way, do you ?" he said, after the consul went, and my rival immediately disavowed any connection with the efforts of the consul. It was my doing, he said,—and the mail carrier scowled at me.

Hour after hour went. It was now noon and I had not eaten since my dinner the previous evening ; but, hungry though I was, I was as keen as ever to get that message from the dead Andree. So I waited while the mail carrier held interview after interview with his friend.

In the meantime, a boy had brought me an answer to a message I had sent to the effect that Carr was holding out for more than was offered, and the reply I received read : "Offer him to five thousand, but secure written guarantee genuine from him."

With this despatch in my hand, I went again to where the two sat dicsussing the matter. "Mr Carr," I said, "I'll give you five thousand for that letter if you come to a lawyer's office with me and write a statement that the thing is genuine."

"Do I have to go to the lawyer's office?" he replied.

"You do," said I.

"Well," he returned, with a smile, "I guess the deal's off. I ain't going to run chances of the pen over this thing, for I guess a paper that'd offer five thou' would put a fellow over the road for fooling 'em. This letter's a thing me and Bill here fixed up at Dawson. We got an old Strand magazine and saw some pictures of letters found on pigeons which returned to Sweden. Bill, he thinks the papers would pay big for a letter from Andree, so we made one. But we've got cold feet now, and the deal's off."

This is why the world was never startled with the news that a letter from Andree had been found in the wilds of Alaska. and the wild tribes of Siberia may still seek for tidings of the lost explorers, as the Czar commanded in the signs which he scattered over the northern wastes.

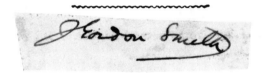

The Canadians at Paardeberg.

It was the night before the final decisive attack upon the larger of the Boer General, Cronje, which resulted in the surrender of the man in whom, on the Western frontier, the enemy placed most reliance, together with some four thousand of his followers.

It was the eve of the anniversary of the British defeat at Majuba Hill eighteen years before. That disasterous event, unavenged as it was, had instilled deeply into the minds of the Dutch all over South Africa a contempt for the military prowess of Great Britain. It was Majuba which practically ended the Frist Boer War with the advantage to the Dutch : it was Paardeberg, with the capture of Cronje's army, which broke the back of resistance against the British advance upon Pretoria, in the Second Boer War.

* * * * * * *

Belmont, Graspan, and Modder River had been at best dearly-bought victories, in which the reckless bravery of the British soldier and his company officers was more than counterbalanced, in the mind of the enemy, by what was regarded as lack of skill in tactics. Magersfontenin, Colense, and Stormberg came in quick succession, with staggering significance to the whole British Empire ; while Boer hope and confidence rose to a dangerous height. The one tiny ray of sunshine, which shot feebly through the black sky of disaster that prevailed during all those weary weeks, was the defeat of the Sunnyside rebels, by Canadian and Australian troops, on the extreme left flank of General Lord Metheun's position on the Modder River.

Weeks passed, and the world waited for the next stroke to cast the balance ! Meantime British troops poured in thousands into Cape Town, as evidence of the anxiety which the chapter of disasters had aroused.

Then came the wonderful mobilization of the army on the Western frontier, under Field Marshal Lord Roberts, the quick march from Enslin, the rendezvous at Ramdam Farm, followed closely by the capture of Jacobsdal with the enemy's hospitals, and Klip Drift with their commissariat: the splended dash of the cavalry, under General Sir John French, for Kimberley, and its relief; and the doubling back of the same weary soldiers to the Modder River, to head off the desperate attempt of the Boer General, Cronje, to make good escape from the now untenable position in the Magersfontein kopjes.

Cornered, with British cavalry spanning the river ahead, and four divisions of infantry slowly but surely encircling him, Cronje and his sturdy burghers were not yet captured. With consumate skill, using to the full the marvellous advantages which the country afforded for a strong defensive position, the Boer leader established his laager at a point where a sharp elbow in the river gave him the protection of high banks on three sides, with a level glacis sloping up from the trenches, on the fourth, for a distance of a mile or more. A plentiful fringe or trees along the river bank afforded a partial screen for the Boer wagons, which were parked within a narrow oblong under cover of trees and scrub. It was shortly after daybreak on Sunday morning, the eighteenth of February, when the British infantry, by a series of forced marches closed in around the enemy's position. For over a mile along the river, either way from the laager, the Boers occupied the banks and numerous deep sluits or dongas extending at right angles from them, in many instance for a quarter of a mile and even more. All day Sunday the British infantry and artillery endeavored to dislodge the enemy from the river banks and dongas, and force them back within the confines of their laager. Just as the day was closing, a general charge was ordered, and the cordon of troops about the laager made a desperate attempt to close in upon the enemy, with the result that something over a thousand officers and men on the British side bit the dust, killed or wounded. Though effectually cornered, the Boers demonstrated that they could still bite with effect, and no further attempts were made to force the issue by infantry advances over open ground, Instead, the artillery fire of the entire force was concentrated upon the laager, and under cover of that fire, for more than a week the nineteenth brigade of the ninth division of infantry, commanded by Brigadier General Smith-Dorrien, assisted by a detachment of the Royal Engineers, slowly sapped up the river bank towards the Boer laager.

* * * * * * * * * *

Monday evening, the twenty sixth of February, the Canadians occupied the forward trenches in front of the enemy's position. We had known all afternoon that some desperate game was on, but those who knew would not tell what it was. A sharp musketry fire was kept up at intervals during the afternoon from the enemy's trenches, which were a bare three hundred yards to our front. A short distance to our rear the Shropshire regiment occupied the second line of trenches, while the Gordon Highlanders manned another trench, extending from that occupied by the Shropshires in the form of an obtuse angle, including towards the front trench at its extremity from the river bank. The further bank of the river, flanking the trench in front, was occupied by a single company of the Canadian regiment.

Finally, just before dark, the orders came. The plan had evidently been carefully conceived, for every company officer received his instructions in writing. At a given hour, between midnight and two o'clock in the morning, the entire regiment was to advance from the forward trenches under cover of the darkness. The front rank was to carry entrenching tools, with their rifles slung, and to advance keeping touch at arms length ; the second rank armed with rifles only, was to follow in the same manner, with an interval of ten paces. Absolute silence was to be maintained, and at the first discharge from the enemy's lines, both ranks were to fall flat upon their faces without returning fire. The Gordon Highlanders in the flank trenches on one side, and the company of Canadians across the river on the other flank, were to answer the Boer fire, and thus cover the silent advance. The Shropshire regiment, occupying the rear trenches, were to act in support. A detachment of the Royal Engineers was to advance at the same time under cover of the high river bank.

The object of the movement was to dig a trench upon a slightly elevated ridge of ground not more than eighty or one hundred yards from the outer entrenchments of the enemy. Success meant that with the dawn the troops occupying the new trench would be able by their fire to make the outer line of the Boer cover untenable, and we knew that their whole system of underground defence was connected by "T" trenches. But the chances of success—well, it was a desperate business at best!

As the night grew apace, and its inky darkness made even the faces of close neighbors nothing more than a dim silhouette, there was a significant silence all along the line ; broken only by an occasional musket shot from other parts of the field. There was no interchange of complimentary remarks, such as are usual among soldiers even in the most dangerous firing line. It was obvious that every man had nerved himself and was silently awaiting the signal. No one who has not waited similarily for an order which involved—perhaps death and disaster ; perhaps a dearly-bought victory—can understand the agonizing torture of those weary hours.

The word came at last, and silently the regiment crawled from cover. Slowly the first, and then the second line, disappeared into the darkness in front. Faintly the sound of marching came back, but it was impossible to see anything. Suddenly, out to the left, came the sharp crack of a single Mauser, followed in an instant by a rattling fire all along the Boer lines. Then came volley, after volley, a perfect hell of fire, which was answered by the Gordons and the company of Canadians on the opposite bank of the river.

It seemed impossible that men could live out there, and yet there were eight hundred in front. Away at the farthest extremity of the advance, in the intervals between the deadly volleys, our man began to retire, and tumbled into the trenches in tens and twenties. Had the whole affair then been a failure, and were these few stragglers all who were left to tell the tale ? No one seemed to know, even those who returned could only say that they had done so under orders. When the enemy's fire slackened a little, it was found that the general advance and the partial gradual retirement was part of the plan, two companies only remaining to excavate the trench, lying flat, and throwing the earth up in front of them. They were assisted by the engineers working from the river bank. The Boers were evidently deceived, for the working party managed, first, to throw up protecting cover, and finally to complete the required trench, which they occupied for the rest of the night. The movement had been a success, but, at that time, no one knew at what cost.

After an anxious, miserable few hours, day at last began to dawn. The Boer fire had altogether ceased. With the clearer light came the reason. Here and there along the enemy's lines could be seen dirty white flags. Cronje had at last surrendered. Paardeberg had been won, and lusty cheers broke from the men who had forced the issue. Slouch-hatted, long-bearded burghers began to appear from the trenches opposite. A few advanced, and in a few minutes victors and vanquished were lraternizing. It was strange to see the good-fellowship which existed between the grimy Canadians soldiers and the rugged unkempt looking burghers who but a few hours before had poured such a storm of lead into one another.

Thus was Majuba avenged on its anniversary, and at small cost in fife, for the Canadians had obeyed orders with the result that the deadly fire passed over them as they lay upon the ground. The twenty or thirty who fell, killed or wounded, met their fate for the most part during the partial retirement.

A Fiji Incident.

(With Apologies to Sir Fielding Clarke.)

"Write within 1000 words an account of the most interesting incident actually experienced in your career!" That's what the Yankees would call a difficult proposition. My ideas of what is interesting may differ entirely with the ideas of the apocryphal Benjamin Binns; however, here goes.

Some few years ago I was Stipendiary Magistrate and Resident Commissioner of the Island of Kadavu; a beautiful Island in the Fiji Group. It was my first magistracy.

One day the Government steamer "Clyde" appeared at Tavuki, the Roko's (native King's) village and my headquarters. The Governor's ensign was flying at the stern, and some bushy-headed fuzzy-wuzzies in Government House uniform, who could be seen on the deck of the vessel, plainly told us that the Governor, the late Sir John Bates Thurston, was aboard.

Before the gubernatorial party can land the usual native ceremonies have to be gone through. The Roko's mata-ni-vanua (herald) swims off unaccompanied to the steamer with the "qaloqalovi." Upon the arrival of a superior chief at any place in Fiji, the omission on the part of the inhabitants to swim off with the "qaloqalovi" would, before annexation, have warranted an attack on the village; when the captured females would have been taken off as slaves by the conquerors and the males would have made "vuaka balavu"---literally "long pig," and been baked and eaten. "Qalo" is the verb to swim, and the custom consists of swimming off with a "tabua" (whale's tooth) which has to be presented. A refusal to accept it would mean hostility.

After clambering aboard with this, the herald crawls up to the Governor on his hands and knees and, sitting on his haunches tailor fashion, claps his hands and grunts, and then proceeds to address the Governor in the usual formula, asking him to be kindly disposed towards them, that the food plantations have yielded but poor crops this year, and they have but little to present as there is scarcity in the land, and to be of good mind and look lightly upon their shortcomings. This finished, he holds the tabua, which is suspended from a piece of sinnet, up to the Governor, who touches it, showing that he accepts it and incidentally their demands. To illustrate the significance of tabuas—pronounced tambuas—I would mention that when the Wesleyan Missionary Baker was killed and eaten in 1876, a tabua was sent ahead of him to a chief in the interior of Vitilevu, with a request from the district where Baker had established himself that he be killed. But for the acceptance of that fatal whale's tooth with the accompanying request, Baker would have survived.

After this the Roko goes off to the steamer in his canoe and surrenders his staff of office to his superior chief, the Governor, which is only handed back to the Roko when the Governor takes his departure from the Roko's territory. The further retention of the staff then would mean the suspension of the Roko from office.

These preliminaries satisfactorily over, the Governor and his party can land without their dignity suffering. They are received on the beach by all the squatting townspeople who "tama" (grunt) as the Governor approaches. "Ai sevu" (First fruits) are then presented. The "first-fruits" consist of squealing pigs, chickens, a turtle or two, piles of fresh-dug yams and taro, and always a root of "kava" (the Piper physticum, from the chewed or pounded root of which the grog of the South Sea Islanders is made). But to get on to my "interesting incident."

Amongst the Governor's party was Sir Fielding Clarke, then Chief Justice of Fiji, now Chief Justice of Jamaica. After dinner, in the cool moonlight of the lovely tropical evening, Sir John and the Chief Justice, accompanied by others, strolled under the cocoanut palms through the village. A large native house was passed where a lot of young fellows could be seen through the wide-open door playing euchre—"cut throat"— on the mats. It is about the only game of cards the natives know, and they often play for hours with greasy cards besmeared with the cocoanut oil with which they anoint their bodies. Beside them was another young fellow making a bowl of " kava." Sir Fielding Clarke detached himself from the party, entered the house, and squatted on the mats to watch the players. They deferentially made way for him, and handed him the first bowl of grog and the concomitant " seluka." "Selukas" are native cigarettes made of tobacco wrapped in dried banana leaf instead of paper. After a while he took a hand in the game of cards and had a second bowl of kava and a second seluka, and rejoined Sir John at a late hour delighted with the evening he had spent. I timidly asked him : " I suppose you know what that big building is, Sir Fielding ? " He said : " What is it ? " I had to tell him : " Why, it's the Provincial Gaol, and those ' good fellows' to whom you refer are the Provincial prisoners ! "

The Chief Justice collapsed, and Sir John roared with laughter at him. It was a standing joke against Sir Fielding as long as he remained in Fiji.

The Devotions of an Emperor.

The Peking cart, an abominable vehicle in the best of weather, jolted and tumbled and bumped and splashed through the foul sea of mud that stretched, inky and noisome, between the low walls flanking the alley-ways or the tightly battened shop fronts that bordered the larger thorough-fares. A lonely light here and there sent its tail of yellow streaking across the rain-swept puddles. Occasionally a cart lurched past us. In the main streets a few coolies, working even at that hour of the night, were putting the finishing touches on the causeway, raised in the centre of the metropolitan road, over which the Yellow Emperor was to pass.

The Llama, true to his word, was waiting at the gate of the Yung Ho Kung, the temple whose seething host of Mongol monks has ever been the nucleus for all anti-foreign demonstrations in the Chinese capital. The priest escorted me to his cell and there we waited during the long hours of the night. Towards three o'clock, the tolling of the bell, solemn, dole-ful, muffled by the drumming of the steady down-pour, called the waiting hundreds to their posts. When the shuffling of countless feet along the path had died away we ventured out, and started for the inner courtyards. Gatemen and guardians had been well bribed to keep the secret, and from a distance it would have been difficult to detect the presence of a stranger. My head had been shorn after much patient clipping with a pair of nail scissors. I wore a purple gown and a fine red sash and my silken trousers were tucked into tall Mongol boots, while the whole was capped with a flat hat of straw, tipped well forward to hide eyes and nose, the most tell-tale features of the foreigner.

We entered a two-storied chapel in the second court. My conductor dared not speak—he drew his hand ominously across his throat and led me up a flight of rickety stairs, then pushed me under an altar at the end of the sombre room, and left me. Tapers, soaked in sesame oil, were flickering before the Asian dieties that were ranged in grim grandeur around the hall. The altar ornaments, gilt lotus flowers, paired fishes, graven flags, stood in gaunt rows. Heaps of cakes, red and white, tempted the Divine appetite ; wine, in the skull-bowls of Thibet, stood ready to quench even a God-like thirst. From the raftered ceiling strange silken scrolls, dusty, worm-eaten, hung like parti-coloured cobwebs.

I ventured from my stifling hiding-place to revel in the wonders of the room ; but e'er half its riddles had been solved, I was scurried back to a corner, there to crouch as a venerable Llama creaked up the stair-way and wandered from altar to altar trimming the lamps. Discovery would have brought down upon me the wrath of the Imperial Body Guard and a foreigner in the vestments of a Mongol priest, his head shaven, would have been deprived of all the glamour that surrounds the sack-coat and pantaloons of the Occident.

The day was breaking. Eunuchs, soldiers, officials, high and low, hurried back and forth in the court below. Matting was laid over the stone flagging ; all was a bustle of preparation. There came the sound of a bugle call from the distance, then the notes of the march that one hears wherever one meets the foreign-drilled troops of China. The Emperor was on his way. Up the steep stairs came the guardian to throw back the doors which opened on the balcony, that no one might peer through a crack in the wood-work on the August Person of His Majesty. Officials inspected the lower room and went on to the temple yards beyond, to make sure that there was no intruder to profane the sanctity of the places to be blessed with the Imperial presence.

Three priests crept up from below and with them I slipped along on my stomach to the edge of the balcony where, through an opening in the carving, I could see all that happened.

From the entrances on the East and West of the courtyard came columns of high priests, venerable men, gray-beards, yellow-robed, gay with red scarf and gilt-lacquered hat, swinging censers or holding their rods of office before them as they marched. They fell back on either side of the stone terrace that fronts the facade of the temple hall. An official advanced, followed by four more priests ; then came the Emperor, slight, boyish, timid he seemed. He looked neither to the right nor to the left, but with measured step walked towards the altar. Nine Princes of the Imperial clan formed his suite and they alone were allowed to accompany him to the great door-way, to stand guard while he made obeisance before the Lord Buddha who grants the blessed rain and gladdens the world with sunshine, who causes the seed to sprout and ripens the golden grain. He prayed, and the priests chanted a deep, solemn, rumbling song, oriental, weird, intoned in Thibetan, the tongue of the Buddhistic saints.

The Emperor passed on under the shadow of the silken hangings through the heavy clouds of incense that filled the sanctuary. The Princes moved forward, the Llamas followed, chanting as they marched, their censers swinging, their gilt hats glistening, their gorgeous robes gleaming in the early morning sunlight. The "Lord of Ten Thousand Years" had recognized the existence of a Divinity, a spiritual power before whom he, the Over-Lord of teeming millions who worship him as something more than human, had thrice bowed his proud head. Through the crevice in the balcony, a wondrous picture in its grotesque frame, a Foreign Devil had seen the Son of Heaven bend a reverential knee.

Impression Pénible.

Impression pénible! oui, très pénible même et cette impression je l'ai eue le samedi 20 février, 1904, à mon arrivée au Japon.

Je pensais trouver la sérénité, l'éternel sourire.........

Je pensais trouver l'orient, le soleil.........

Je pensais trouver le Japon enfin! J'ai trouvé la guerre, des bruits de torpilles, j'ai trouvé la neige, la pluie ; j'ai trouvé " Influenza."

C'est le Koréa qui m'amena du pays du soleil, j'ai nommé la Californie, dans le pays du froid.

Je me promenais donc a travers le monde comme une croute de pain derrière une malle, ne pensant à rien, quand un coup de canon vint troubler ma sérénité. Le Koréa stopait immédiatement, un homme de guerre nous barrait la route..........

Le charme était rompu, mon pendule était détraqué, la croute de pain n'était plus derrière la malle.........

En mettant le pied sur la terre Japonaise, mon pas était mal assuré et la Jinrikisha que je pris, s'en allait en zigzaguant comme une petite personne ivre, sans avoir aucun scrupule pour mes pauvres os. C'est que son âme, sa petite âme de Jinrikisha, s'en était allée et suivait, la bas, la grande guerre.

En allant de Yokohama à Tokyo dans un de ces élégants compartiments de 1ere classe, emmené à toute vitesse (3 Km. à l'heure) par une locomotive hurlante et soufflante, un jeune Japonais très bien mis et qui nous égaya pendant tout le trajet par une toux m'alodieuse, m'adressa la parole dans sa langue natale. Je crus comprendre qu'il me presentait à une charmante petite geisha assise à ses cotés.

J'avoue que ma première impression fut plutôt mauvaise, pénible même..... Cependant à la longue, ma curiosité l'emporta et je me fis répéter son nom:

"Influenza."

Ne trouvez-vous pas que ce nom a comme un certain goût de terroir?

Avec ma vive imagination et me rappelant les délicieux romans de Pierre Loti, je vis dans ce nom tout un poéme et je me pris à supposer qu'il signifiait " Fleur de Lotus."

Hélas! mon poéme fut court et j'appris bien vite que " Influenza " voulait dire " Fleur de bronchite."

Mais cette petite personne occupait déjà mon cerveau et mes pensées. Le dirais-je! des frissons secouaient mon corps tout entier, mes jambes se dérobaient sous moi, ma gorge me chatouillait désagréablement, j'étais pincé! Depuis cette heure elle ne me quitta plus, s'attacha à mes pas, ne me laissant, inexorable, aucun moment de répit. Je n'ai plus qu'une idée, la fuir. Koréa pour moi, comme pour les Japonais, est devenu synomyme de "terre promise," et je m'entends souvent murmurer:" " Je voudrais bien y aller."

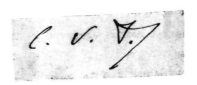

How I Selected a Campaign Outfit.

I have been asked to write about my most interesting experience as a newspaper man. It would be difficult for me to select the most interesting experience I have met with since I have been a member of the profession. I have had many interesting experiences, which vary all the way from assisting a trio of medical students rob a graveyard to watching soldiers kill one another.

Up to the time I arrived in Tokyo I was inclined to believe that the most interesting experience that ever befell me was when I was called out of a box seat at a circus in Shanghai, China, and asked to officiate as referee o a wrestling bout between a professional strong man and a heavyweight pugilist. I was well aware, after I had given the decision against the prize-fighter, that it was an occasion fairly teeming with interest. And, judging from the vociferous manner in which the male portion of the audience demanded another instalment o the performance, I felt quite sure that they too were interested in what the demonstrator of the manly art of self-defense did to me.

But during the time I have been in Tokyo awaiting permission to go to the front, I have concluded that my most interesting experience has been in getting a field outfit together.

I was in the Philippine Islands when the Japanese started in to polish off the Russians, and as soon as I could find a steamer that was bound this way, I packed up my tools and hied me henceward.

Before I arrived I was under the impression that I could go to the scene of carnage with the field equipment I brought from Manila, and which I had always found to be ample for the needs of any war correspondent. It consisted mainly of a tin mess pan, a pair of leather leggins, a tooth brush and a lead pencil. But before I had been in the capital ten minutes I discovered that I knew nothing at all about it.

Several good friends told me that I would have to join the " Ah Shing Cadets," which, upon inquiry, I learned was the official name given the correspondents because a Chinese tailor named Ah Shing was assisting them to expand their expense accounts by furnishing them with a sort of orphan school uniform made of corduroy, and by courtesy called a riding suit.

I joined the cadets, but the minute I clothed myself in the corduroy riding suit it struck me that there was something lacking.

After several minutes of heart to heart talk with my fellow cadets I learned what was needed to fill the aching void. It was a saddle. I bought one.

Quite naturally, a saddle is not of much use without a horse, unless it is used to trim a Christmas tree. So I decided to buy a horse.

Before I started out to become the owner of a horse I had no idea that in all the world there were as many horses as were offered me. Every other man I met had a horse that was of great value to him, but which he was ready to part with if I thought I could use the animal in rushing news back from the front.

Now, if there is anything in this world which I know absolutely nothing about it is a horse. If I started out to become the owner of a street-car or even a hearse, I might be able to make a fair bargain. But a horse—well, a horse is the limit.

Of all the horses I inspected the one that looked best to me was a little spotted China pony which I found at Yokohama. I had made up my mind to buy him when I was informed that he was a racing pony that had been brought to Yokohama to do great things on the race track. I learned, also, that he had done things on the track, but they were not of sufficient greatness to induce bettors to invest in tickets on him the second time. So I did not buy him. I am willing to go to war on horseback, but I'll be everlastingly condemned if I'll go into battle on the back of a second hand racehorse.

But I bought a horse this morning. Since I have owned him several well meaning war correspondents have told me that he has a few defects, among them being a lame leg ; but that is not worrying me at all, for any fool can see that he still has three good legs.

Up to date I have a riding outfit and a horse to go with it, a tent with my name on it in freight car letters, and a few tons of miscellaneous paraphernalia, and am now negotiating the purchase of a watchdog. I do not know why I should go to war with a watchdog, but on the other hand I have been unable to find anyone who can give me any valid reason why I should not take one.

My field outfit is almost complete. In checking over a memorandum of the things I have been told to provide myself with, I find I have procured everything except a pianola, alarm clock, ice-cream freezer, lace curtains for the tent, chestnut roaster, easy chair, umbrella, and a safety deposit vault for the dog.

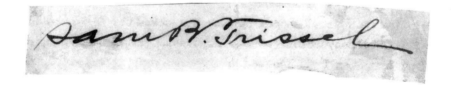

Sognando !

Mia amata, dolcissima Ersilia,

È solamente mezz'ora che mi son levato dal letto e ti scrivo. Ti scrivo mentre fuori tutto é silente ; tutto dorme ancora nella quiete ! Il Sole, facendo capolino dalle vette delle lontane montagne, viene a baciare, con i suoi raggi dorati, le corolle dischiuse al bacio della tenue mattinata primaverile e la pallida luna piegando semprepiù ad ovest, viene a rischiarare la finestra tua.

Mentre scrivo tu dormi ; dormi un sonno di pace e quiete, felice e tranquillo !.........

Non tenermi il broncio se stavolta non mi servo di parole amorose ; se non ti ripeto ancora che t'amo tanto e tanto, mia dolcissima.

No ; permettimi che non ti ripeti le sole parole che le labbra sappiano pronunziare ; permetti che stavolta—per questa volta sola—ti racconto quanto ho sognato. Ascolta :

Era tardi iersera quando sfogliavo l'ultima pagine del " *Things Japanese* " di Chamberlain. I rintocchi dell' orologio a campana m'annunziavano le due. Ero stanco ; aveo letto abbastanza e non appena girai la chiavetta della lampadina elettrica, mi addormentai.

E sognai ; sognai trovarmi a Pechino, durante la rivolta dei Boxers.

Eravamo rifugiati nella nostra Legazione, ove trovavansi poche provvigioni alimentarie ed una assai povera cantina.

Il saperci assediati, non era che l'ultima nostra preoccupazione. Conoscevamo i Chinesi ; il sapevamo incapaci di quanto malauguratamente oprarono e passavamo i nosti giorni in splendite colazioni e pranzi luculliani.

Ma ben presto le alimentarie volsero al termine e così pure la cantina.

Le comunicazioni telegrafiche con Tientsin, essendo interrotte, non ci davano alcuna opportunità di ricevere soccorsi.

Così passammo quasi un mese dopo del quale alla noncuranza subentrò il panico ; al sorriso la mestizia, alla speranza lo sconforto !.........

Quando l'ultimo biscotto fu consumato, passammo alla Legazione d'Inghilterra.

Chi dimenticherà più quei giorni trascorsi non ad altro che a continue fucilate contro i ribelli ?

Chi dimenticherà quelle persone che, avventuratesi fuori della Legazione, non ritornarono più ?

Chi potrà obbliare quei volti di bimbi innocenti, pallidi, sconvolti, terrorizzati, stretti al petto delle loro mamme, che ad ogni colpo di moschetto, davano in pianti e sussulti ? Chi potrà piu cancellare dal cuore quelle espressioni di dolori, quelle lagrime che, irrigando il viso delle tenere madri, cadevano sul capo delle loro creature sparute ?

Io non potrò enumerarti, Ersilia dolcissima, quante centinaie di proiettili nemici si conficcavano nelle mura del nostro ricovero ; ma dovea no essere parecchie.

I nosti colpi erano inoffensivi certamente, dappoichè non scorgevamo i ribelli che, provvisti di ottimi *watterly*—ultimo modello—ed alcuni vecchi cannoni, eseguivano tiri di precisione.

Quando, giungendo la sera, il fuoco cessava, stanchi, sfiniti, esausti di forze e speranze, lasciavamo il nostro posto di combattimento, per passare al *dining-room*, non avevamo altro pasto che della carne marcita di cavallo e raramente un pezzo di cane arrosto !.........

Io avevo completamente perduto lo stomaco, e la gola era ribelle a far passare questo cibo tuttaltro che delicato. Un' altra settimana ancora che si fosse prolungato l'assedio, sarei morto certamente.

Dei Chinesi—fedeli ai loro padroni—ogni giorno venivano ad anunziarci l'arrivo dei soldati ; ma dall'alba sino a quando il Sole si coricava dietro i colli lontani, nessuno giungeva !.........

Un mattino, quando i colpi di moschetto fischiavano numerosi, giunsero nel cortile i soliti *boics* gridando : *The soldiers, the foreign soldiers.*

Era il medesimo annunzio quotidiano al quale da tempo non davamo più ascolto.

Ma dopo pochi minuti, come per incantesimo, il fuoco nemico era cessato, e dal Canale Imperiale i soldati entravano in Pechino. Primi fra essi i Giapponesi, che, accolti a fucilate dai boxers, impavidi, avanzando, venivano a liberarci!.........

Lasciammo la Legazione ed uniti ai soldati mettemmo in fuga il nemico che, accoccolato nei tetti delle loro catapecchie, tiravano su noi a mezzo d'un buco praticato fra i mattoni.

Accadde un massacro!.........Ogni cavallo trovato, divenne proprietà di noialtri borghesi che in pattuglie di dieci o dodici, scorazzavamo le praterie sconfinando i ribelli.

Della mia piccola brigata ero l'ultimo, essendo il mio cavallo vecchio, debole e malconcio abbastanza.

Ero lontano dai miei compagni un trecento metri, quando la mia bestia, ricevendo un proiettile nella spalla sinistra, cadde come fulminato.

Nella caduta sentii spezzarmi una gamba e non avevo ancora tentato d'alzarmi, quando un *Boxer* di corsa s'avvia verso di me, con la sciabola squainata. Il suo viso era tanto orribile, da incutere paura al solo guardarlo. Tolgo la mia rivoltella dal fodero e mirandogli al petto ero per far partire il colpo, quando un altro Chinese mi assesta uua sciabolata alla testa.

Il sangue m' innonda il viso ; cado agonizzante!.................

In questo momento il mio *boy* bussando alla porta della camera entra portandomi il mattutino caffe ; ma resta come esterefatto !

Dai capelli mi colava sul guanciale e sul viso ancora l'acqua della bottiglia preparata sul comodino, mentre nella destra impugnavo la candela.

Aveo sognato dell' assedio del 1900 !.................

Saved by a Desert Quail.

It was a mere incident, just a bit out of the " damnable ordinary," quite unimportant to all the world excepting only to Carmelita, me—and the rattlesnake.

I had been " riding slanting" for days toward the scene of the threatened outbreak among the long-suffering tribe of Copah Indians, on the edge of the yellow Mojave desert, in the Land Where it is Always Afternoon. If you ask me about it, I will tell you that I afterward reached the ruction-center in time to see the bedevilled aborigines kick up a deal of dust and trouble, attended their war councils, slept in their pole romadas for many weeks, and trekked with the dusky, baffled exiles westward to a point where Greed and Chicane may not again steal their poor homes, which had been theirs " ever since God made the Mesa Grande ; " but all that is a longer and a very different story.

For many months, for health's sake, I had been doing my editorial work in the saddle and by the lonely desert and mountain trail. I was also a United States Ranger in charge of a district of the Forest Reserve, comprising the whole of La Liebre mountain range and a fraction of the Great Thirst Land, to the east, where Nature no longer displays maternal tenderness, but shows herself only a niggardly and austere stepmother.

A week before, the captain of our Rangers had requested me to explore that unknown region and to blaze a trail, on my way to the Agua Caliente Indian villages of adobe ; and this is what happened to me after I had lost my canteen on one of the hottest reaches of those 20,000 square miles of the Devil's Back Yard.

With a silk handkerchief tied over my nostrils to keep the bitter alkali dust out, for three days I and Carmelita had " bucked " the barbed chemi-sal and mesquite and fought through the daggered yuccas and leathery manzanita. Over the blistering sands, up and down the baking shoulders of the vast huddle of granite giants, now picking our way wearily and gingerly over the loose rubble of a a dead watercourse gloomed in by the walls of a mile-deep cañon, now toiling up and up, along the bony spine of a thin " hogback " or mountain ridge, as peaked as the letter A and with the sharp up-swing of Fujiyama, we struggled, the thermometer crawling from 100 degrees in the morning to 120 at noon.

Here were no mountains in emerald coronation robes, but only waterless desert-stuff piled high, shimmering in eternal silence, relieved by clumps of dusty greasewood chaparral and cacti, and spanned by a sky of hot brass.

To the north and west, for a hundred miles, rose crest on crest of jagged yellow peaks, buttressed by long " hogbacks " of decomposed granite. To the east, seen through the notches of the ridges, cut by dry arroyo-beds and studded thinly with fantastic, twisted yucca-palms, the palpitating desert stretched, baked and flat, out to the far rim of the world. Southward, somewhere beyond this vast audience chamber of Satan, lay the Copah Indian village — and perhaps my deliverance; *quien sabe* ? Two days without food or water, I had zig-zagged with my led bronco up and down milehigh chunks of desert, belched up and forgotten by Pluto, and left there on edge, hot, lawless, fantastically chaotic, unexplored, dead.

The year was at its hottest. Game there was none. I had insulted my stomach with sundry offerings of young and bitter chilicothe tubers and handfuls of sour, juiceless manzanita berries. All day long, to bring moisture, I had rolled a pebble in my dry mouth.

Not a sign of life had I seen for three weary days, save two horrible carrion-ravens that followed like silent demons and perched to shake the white dust from their ebon shoulders, and leered evilly at the spent bronco and famishing rider, and followed again—and waited—waited. There was never a bird-note, nor the track of a deer or a puma, but only the blinking of the horned toad and the petulant buzz of the great, fat rattlesnake.

Too spent at last to walk, I clung weakly to the saddle horn, swaying, my head drooping lower and lower. The pebble dropped out of my mouth, hot and dry. Still my pretty mare plowed heroically through the sand along the roof of the ridge. The buttes and the sky grew blurred and darker, though I knew that the sun was still beating down fiercely.

Presently we stumbled over portions of a human mummy, some gray rags, and the rotten wreck of a Spencer rifle. Had that dead Thing, too, once fought the battle with the desert, and babbled of cool groves and plashing streams? Had he, too, gone mad with listening to the growing clangor and boom of that infernal Silence? Had he dug his bleeding finger stumps into the blistering gravel, moaning thickly over his blackened tongue, " Agua! Madre de Dios! Agua "?

Faugh! It is enough to nerve one to conquer Hades. On I toiled, my poor beast following in pathetic trustfulness.

You must know that in the Great Thirst Land there is no moisture in the air to make dew for the fevered night, and that all the day the fierce heat sucks one's very marrow dry as a sponge, so that though he drink every half hour, the traveler is always athirst. Gods! How many days since we had tasted water—I and Carmelita?

I felt the desert madness coming on, and fought it. I knew that yonder cool lake with its fronded margin, that glimmered beyond the red buttes to the East was a mirage. I knew that the Devil's Tattoo which roared in my ears was the subconscious " Taranta—taranta—taranta " of death. My tongue, blackened and swollen, filled my throat, and thrust out between my cracked lips.

The Thirst Land swung 'round and 'round. The world turned black. I clutched ineffectually at Carmelita's neck and shoulder, and fell, with my face in the sand.

A loud, angry " Sk-r-r-r! " within a yard of my head galvanized me into life. It was the challenge of the deadly rattlesnake; but that buzz meant not death, but hope of life to me! I sprang to my knees. I hurled down a rock into the great yellow coil. Half stunned, he writhed down the steep cañon side. I crawled after, and despatched him; and I remember laughing aloud as I ripped the mottled skin from his sides. Crawling back, I secured a stewpan from my saddlebags, built a fire of dead mesquite sticks, cut the five-foot Terror of the Desert into short sections, and in ten minutes was tearing the great, half-broiled and steaming morsels with my teeth. Never was there tender cutlet or fricasseed quail so sweet of savor as that fried rattlesnake. The flesh was white, tough, and a bit stringy, but it was full of oil, and it meant life.

Strengthened, I removed the heavy saddle, and caressed the poor mare. Her fine eyes were dull, her head low, so that her long, wavy mane swept the sand. Feebly she tried to nibble the dead tops of a clump of wild buckwheat, but the wiry shreds fell out of her mouth, dry.

On we toiled again, till at nightfall we reached the sheer end of the ridge. Despair seized me when I saw that three sides were almost as steep as a Queen Anne roof, and half a mile to the bowlder wash at the base. We must go back.

I tossed on my blanket till midnight when the sands cooled, and I slept, dreaming of Dante in hell. In the morning I saw that Carmelita had not moved out of her tracks. Blood red and fiercely hot, at half-past five the sun leaped over the dun crags and I knew that I must find a spring of water that day or Carmelita and I had seen our last sunrise. " At any rate," I reflected, grimly, " I shall have this cosmic cemetery all to myself, and escape a lying epitaph."

Suddenly my despair was changed to joy. I heard afar down the cañon a faint, mellow " O-hi-o ! O-hi-o ! " as pleasant as a " Good morning "* from a pretty musume in Tokyo. It was the clear, far call of the California valley quail—and it said to ears versed in desert-craft, " Here is water ! " For let me tell you that where the quail is at dawn, there is water.

I tried to urge my mare toward the sound, but she would not lift a hoof. She was " all in." Seizing a tin can I plunged down the declivity. In a clump of alders hidden by crags, half a mile below, I found the life-giving waters bubbling up, clear and free as Truth. I felt like erecting a shrine there and worshipping Water. Never before had I known its meaning. Filling my can and my sombrero, I toiled painfully and carefully up the rocky acclivity, carrying life to Carmelita. Three times I repeated the trip. Then, making a long detour I brought her down to the spring.

---

* The Japanese word for "Good morning' is pronounced "O-hi-o."

As we approached the little pool, there stood cocky little Tassel Top on one foot, searching me with innocent, inquiring eye, ignorant of the savagery of civilized man, therefore unafraid. Impelled by the brute instinct of hunger, I jerked my carbine from the saddle-scabbard, while my mare, her nose thrust half to the eyes into the pool, drank greedily; levelled it at Don Chiquito Quail, and then lowered it, ashamed.

"No, little O-hi-o," I said, aloud, "you have saved our lives. Life is as sweet to you as to me. Go in peace; and like Abou Ben Adhem, may your tribe increase." He ran off, clucking and bowing, and the ravens wheeled away to the Thirst Land.

Then, while my bronco munched the scant salt grass, I picked the semi-circular bones out of what was left of my fried rattlesnake, munched the tough white fiber, and afterward lay for an hour with my chin on my fists, staring, wide-eyed and wider-souled, into the heart of the pool—into new and vaster heavens—and was content.

A Boxer Charge.

Under the ancient walls of the Tayar city towards the end of the unique campaign of 1900, a column of German infantry, with baggage and provisions for a three day's expedition, is slowly moving through the heavy sand in a southwesterly direction. It is a cold morning with a tinge of dampness in the air and the smart German officers in their delicate grey blue military cloaks buttoned up at the throat seem somewhat out of keeping with their surroundings the yellow-faced convoy drivers and their dingy little ponies.

The Allies occupy the Chinese Capital, the court has fled and all fears of a yellow peril war has again died away. The incident I am about to relate can only claim attention from the fact of it being an aspect of warfare now fast disappearing, a charge of fanatical fighting men of the most ancient civilisation ; poor volunteers, for that is what the Boxers were, members of secret societies who had sworn to drive the foreign devils into the sea ; who with their homemade swords and old rifles made a desperate charge on the ranks of the best disciplined troops of Europe.

The column started this morning with the object of destroying one of the last bands of Boxers To hold together since the relief of Peking. We had information that they held a village on the south of Hunting Park, where game was formerly preserved for the sport of the Emperors of China Our road lay through fields of giant millet or kowliang, growing to a height of 10 or 12 feet, Indian corn and other crops mostly lying rotting on the ground for the want of reaping. The villages we came upon were for the most part deserted, except a few old people too feeble to flee and the pariah dogs who in the midst of desolation were thriving. Two days passed in this marching through the country collecting and burning quantities of arms and ammunition found in the villages, but no sign of the Boxers till the afternoon of the third day found us on our way back, with little prospect of coming upon them. The column was marching through the desolate cornfields by the narrow tracks and occasional open clearings. I think we had forgotten all about the object of the expedition when we were without any warning greated by a sharp cracking of rifle fire and almost immediately found ourselves in a large clearing and facing us the whole band of the Boxers, with the low wall of the Hunting Park on our left front lined with the Chinese riflemen in their glowing red turbans, thrown in strong relief by the setting sun. A detachment of the Germans was immediately told off to settle accounts with the men behind the wall, while the troops I accompanied, drawn up in close order with the German flag planted in the centre, were replying to the rifles of our enemy in the clearing. After about an hour of desultory firing on both sides, the whole remaining band of Boxers, leaving all cover that they had been availing themselves of, banded together without any appearance of order or method, with their huge black and white banners inscribed with Chinese characters waving above them and, led by a big Manchu on a rough Chinese pony, they advanced on the Germans. What an extraordinary scene, banners, swords and rifles all mixed together, the dull blue of their peasants, costume relieved by the brilliant scarlet sashes and turbans which made up their uniform, their yellow faces gleaming in the setting sun, distorted with savage cries only a mob rushing to their death. For why should they fear? Each man carries in this sash strips of yellow paper carefully wrapped up and covered with mystic characters blessed by their priests which they firmly believe will render them impervious to the bullets of the foreign devils. After the first volley poured into them half of them were no more. Another volley found the now darkening cornfield covered with heaps of red and blue cloth mixed up with pikes and banners. The whole thing was like a dream it was over so quickly. An hour afterward we were cooking our evening meal in their village, their ghastly painted gods from the Joss house forming the fuel for our campfires.

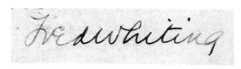

"What about my camp canteen?"

"Four Stone Ten."

" Each correspondent will be allowed baggage not exceeding eight
" kwan (four stone ten pounds) in weight." Extract from letter address-
ed by the Chief of Staff to Foreign War Correspondents.

'Twas a sprightly correspondent and he met me in the Strand,
" Will you come with me across the sea to happy Jappy-land ? "
Now I went with he across the sea, but, here's a funny thing—
In Tokyo, you know, he had another song to sing :

" O it's column one, and column two, and where the deuce am I ?
" And will the office raise the dibs ? and is the climate dry ?
" And what about my camp canteen ? and how, and where, and when.
" Can any fellow see the blessed show on four stone ten " ?

I soothed him with Manhattans while he drew me up a list
Of things that must accompany the errant journalist,
There were shovels, spades, and pickaxes, a patent stove or two,
A cottage tent a regiment could march in column through,
Canned goods galore, of boots a score of pairs of quaint design
From Veltschoen of the Burgher type to felt shoes number nine ;
Six suits of clothes for Manchu snows that cost a tidy yen-
I told him he must work his kit to tally four stone ten.

He took me to his room, and showed a pet contrivance which
With skilled manipulation would work without a hitch,
He fondled natty sketching gear, and shed a tear upon
A telescopic washandstand he'd bought in Oregon.
He'd a bedstead and patent chair, collapsible no doubt-

And a mile of butter muslin to keep mosquites out;
His undergarments would suffice a dozen healthy men—
I told him he must boil it down, and carry four stone ten.

    * * * * * * *

Somewhere near the Yalu River I met him once again,
Outside the Field Post Office, sitting in the mud and rain,
With the regulation bandage on his European arm,
And on his mud-bespattered face a smile of pious calm;
His breath was short from running, though he carried little load
Beyond a Colt revolver, and a map to show the road,
And an old colonial haversack where, hidden sung and warm,
Lay a dozen army biscuits and a crumpled cable form.
I asked him where his outfit was : he answered with a grin—
" A squad of Cossacks left me just what I'm-sitting in :
" But let them keep my patent duds and raid till all is blue ;
" I've gathered in the rarest scoop and the Censor's passed it through!"

" O its column this and column that, and what's the odds at all ?
" You can stick it out on little when your back's against the wall,
" But, if you meet the convoy when you are going back again,
" Just tell them I'd be precious glad to get that four stone ten ! "

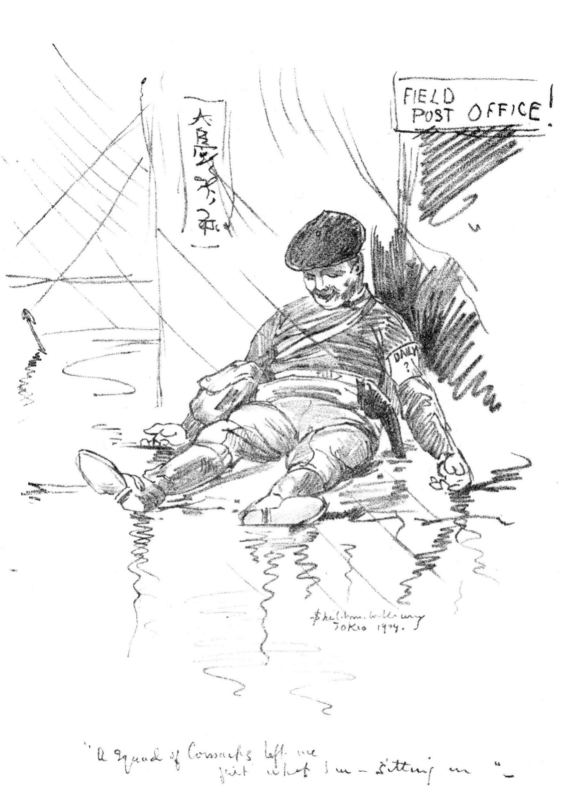

FIELD POST OFFICE!

大島圭介

"A squad of Cossacks left me just where I am — sitting on"

APPENDIX 1

Translation of C. Victor Thomas's "Impression Pénible" by Carey Cupit

Painful impression! Yes, very painful indeed, and I had this impression on Saturday, the 20th of February, 1904, upon my arrival in Japan.

I thought I would find serenity, the eternal smile . . .

I thought I would find the orient, the sun . . .

I thought I would finally find Japan! I found the war, the sound of torpedoes, I found snow, rain; I found "Influenza."

It's Korea that brought me from the country of the sun, named California, to the country of cold.

I was trotting across the world as though I were crusts of bread falling aimlessly from a hamper of food, when cannon fire disrupted my serenity. Korea halted that immediately, a man of war was blocking our route . . .

The charm was broken, my watch was on the blink, no longer was I a crust of bread.

Upon setting foot on Japanese soil, my steps were rather unsure, and the Jinrikisha that I took conducted itself in a zigzag pattern like a little drunk person, without having any scruples for my poor bones. It's that his soul, his little Jinrikisha soul, went away, and following that, over there, was the big war.

It was going from Yokohama to Tokyo in one of these elegant first-class compartments, brought to high speed (3 km an hour) by a huffing and screaming locomotive, a young and very well dressed Japanese person brightened up our journey with a dreadful cough, and addressed me in his native language. I believed that he was going to introduce me to a charming little geisha seated nearby.

I admit that my first impression was rather terrible, painful even . . . Yet in the long run, my curiosity got the better of me and I found myself repeating his name:

"Influenza."

Do you not find that this name has a certain rural taste?

With my active imagination recalling the delicious novels of Pierre Loti, I saw in this name an entire poem and I took to supposing that it meant, "Lotus Flower."

Alas! My poem was cut short and I quickly learned that "Influenza" means "Bronchitis Flower."

But this little person was already occupying my brain and my thoughts. I tell you! The shivers ran through my entire body, my legs gave way beneath me, my throat tickled disagreeably; I was pinched! Since that time it has not left me, attaching itself to my steps, never leaving me, inexorable, no moment of respite. I was left with but one idea, to flee. Korea for me, as for the Japanese, had become synonymous with "the promised land," and I often hear myself murmur: "I would very much like to go there."

APPENDIX 2

DREAMING!

Translation of Alberto Troise's "Sognando!" by Dennis G. Martinez

My Love, sweetest Ersilia,

It's only been a half an hour since I've been out of bed, and I write to you. I write to you while outside everything is silent; everything sleeps in the calm. The Sun peaks out from the summit of the far off mountains; it comes to kiss with its golden rays; the corollas are open to the kiss of the soft Spring morning and the pale moon pushing ever so further to the west, it comes to illuminate your window.

While I write, you sleep; you sleep a sleep of peace and calm, happy and tranquil.

Don't be upset if I am not offering amorous words; if I don't repeat to you again that I love you so much, my sweetest.

No; allow me not to repeat the only words my lips are accustomed to pronouncing; allow me this time, just this one time—I will tell how I dreamt of you. Listen:

It was late yesterday evening when I was leafing through the last pages of Chamberlin's "Things Japanese." The strokes of the clock announced to me that it was two o'clock. I was tired; I had read quite a bit, and I had not even turned off the electric lamp switch, and I had fallen asleep.

I dreamt; I dreamt I was in Peking, during the Boxer Rebellion.

We found refuge in our Legation, where one could find little food and a bleak wine cellar.

Being besieged was the least of our concerns. We were familiar with the Chinese; we knew them to be incapable of harm as they worked so poorly. Despite the circumstances we managed to pass our days in splendid breakfasts and lavish lunches with what was available to us.

But soon food came to an end and the wine as well. The telegraphic communications with Tientsin having been interrupted, we had no opportunity to ask for help.

We went on like this for a month and soon panic set in; Dismay, Hope and Discomfort rejoiced in our presence! . . .

When the last cookie was consumed, we went to the English Legation.

Who can forget that those days we lived through were nothing but continuous shooting at the rebels?

Who can ever forget those people who ventured out of the Legation, never to return?

Who can forget those faces of the innocent children, pale, shocked, terrorized, clinging to the bosom of their mothers, every shot of the muskets, making them jump and cry? Who can obliterate from their hearts those expressions of pain, those tears that irrigated the faces of the tender mothers and fell on their lean creatures?

I can't count, sweetest Ersilia, how many hundreds of enemy fire landed in the walls of our refuge, but it had to be an impressive amount.

Our shots were surely ineffective against the rebels who were equipped with excellent *watterlys*—the latest model—and some old cannons that they shot accurately.

At the arrival of evening, the shooting would cease. Tired, undone, exhausted of strength and hope, we would leave our combat posts, so to go to the *dining room.* We had nothing else to eat but some rotten horse meat and rarely a piece of dog roast! . . .

I had completely lost my appetite, and my throat rebelled against this food that was anything but delicate. Had the siege continued yet for one more week, I would have certainly died.

The Chinese—loyal to their masters—every day came to announce to us the arrival of reinforcements; from sunrise until the Sun would lay behind the distant hills, no one arrived! . . .

One Morning, when the shots of the muskets whistled continuously, and the usual *boys yelled: The soldiers, the foreign soldiers.*

It was the same quotidian announcement to which we no longer paid any attention.

But after a few minutes, almost by enchantment, enemy fire ceased, the soldiers entered Peking along the Imperial Way. The first among them were the Japanese; they were greeted by shots from the Boxers; fearless, they advanced; they were coming to free us! . . .

We left the Legation and joined with the soldiers to rout the enemy who crouched on the roofs of their dilapidated dwellings. They were throwing bricks down at us through holes.

A massacre occurred! . . . Every horse became the property of us, the bourgeoisie. In patrols of ten or twelve, we ran through the fields dispersing the rebels.

I was the last one in my small brigade, because my horse was old, weak and pretty out of shape.

I was about three hundred meters from my companions, when my beast took a projectile in his left shoulder. It fell as if struck by lightning.

In the fall I felt my leg break. I had not yet attempted to get up when a *Boxer* came running toward me, saber pointed.

His face was so horrible that it instilled fear just looking at it.

I pulled out my revolver from the holster and pointed it at his chest to fire a shot, when another Chinese slashed on my head.

Blood flowed down my face; I fell in agony! . . .

At this point my *boy* was knocking on the door of the room bringing me my morning coffee; but he was horrified! . . .

The water from the bottle that was on the bedside table was running down my hair and face onto the pillow, while in my right hand I was clenching the candle.

I had dreamt the siege of 1900! . . .